ANSTEY'S ABBEYS

The crossing tower at Winchester.

The north cloister walk at Canterbury

Opposite: The refectory doorway at Fountains.

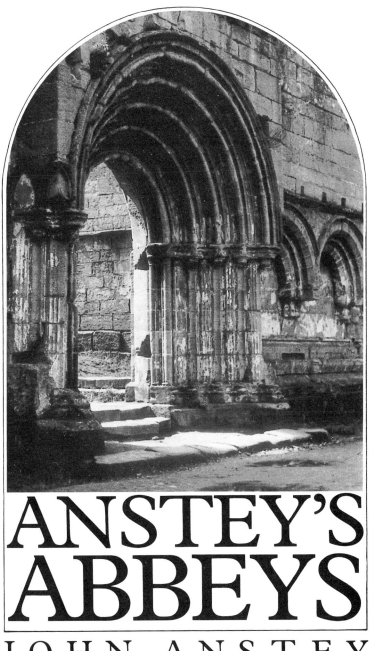

ANSTEY'S ABBEYS

JOHN ANSTEY

Surveyors Publications
12 Great George Street London SW1P 3AD

The east end at Tynemouth

Published on behalf of
The Royal Institution of Chartered Surveyors
by Surveyors Publications
12 Great George Street, London SW1P 3AD

Scottish Branch Office
7 Manor Place, Edinburgh EH3 7DN

ISBN 0 85406 337 4

All photographs by the author
All line drawings by Michael Evans
Design by Tom Deas

Printed in England by
Jolly & Barber Ltd, Rugby, Warwickshire

Contents

	Page
Introduction	7
Why Look at Abbey Ruins?	8
The Abbey as a Whole	10
The Abbey Church	12
The Cloister	30
Some Slypes	34
Libraries and Book Cupboards	36
The Chapter House	38
The Warming House	48
The Refectory	50
The Lavatorium	54
The Kitchen	58
The Lay Brothers' or Cellarers' Range	62
The Day Stair	68
The Dormitory	70
The Reredorter	74
Various Other Rooms	76
The Infirmary	78
The Abbot's Lodging	80
Outbuildings	84
Gatehouses	90
Guest Houses	94
Charterhouses	96
A Short History of the English Monastery	100
Present-Day Monasteries	106
Selective Gazetteer	109
Selective Bibliography	119

Introduction

The east end of Whitby

This is very much a personal guide to what I like looking at in abbeys (priories, nunneries, etc.) that I have enjoyed visiting. It grew out of a series of lectures that I have given to Townswomen's Guilds, Rotary Clubs and the like, in which I have tried to explain to people who are generally alert and interested in things, just what enjoyment there is to be had out of wandering around ruins: indeed, I wanted to call this book *Enjoying Abbeys*. The lectures in turn started because two friends of mine, Joan and Alfred Read, one day asked me what I looked for when visiting sites. On my next visit they came with me, and I found that I got even more pleasure out of trying to explain and to share my interest.

I repeat, then, that this is neither a disinterested nor a comprehensive study. It is one man's individual response to one aspect of an enormous subject.

Why Look at Abbey Ruins?

or some reason which I can't quite explain, though it may be connected with the Victorianisation of almost all complete churches, I find a monastic ruin much more evocative than even the most splendid cathedral, as long as there are enough stones standing one upon another for me to be able mentally to reconstruct some sort of building. When I first used to lecture on abbeys, I used to point to Mattersey Priory as an example of a long detour to see very little. Growing fanaticism on my part has since led me into far longer detours to see far less but, of course, the more you know about the subject the more hope there is that some small fragment will yield something of interest.

It is a little difficult to recreate the secluded, withdrawn, silent atmosphere of Rievaulx or Fountains amid a Bank Holiday crowd, but I think it's easier there and then than in Durham or Canterbury Cathedrals. Don't think I shan't encourage you to go and see those two, however. It was Durham that first really interested me in cathedrals and architecture, and from which my interest in abbeys eventually sprang. At Canterbury, which has enormous interest of its own, including the site of England's most famous martyrdom, there is also the earliest English monastery of all, seen by perhaps less than point one per cent of those who visit its more famous neighbour. St Augustine's Abbey was founded in 598, five hundred years before Christ Church Cathedral began to be built in its present form.

'But what is there to see, what will interest me?' you may ask. *Tot homines, quot sententiae* is a favourite Latin tag of mine, and very appropriate to the Latin-speaking and writing monastic world. A different opinion for every man, might be a rough translation (literally: how many men, so many opinions). Some people will undoubtedly want to recapture an echo of the faith which led so many men and women to spend their lives in more or less solitary and silent communion with God. Architectural historians will try to see the development of different styles, from the austere and simple Norman (my own favourite, as it happens) through to the ornate fan vaulting of the fifteenth and sixteenth centuries, just before the Dissolution. Social historians will want to trace the influence of the monasteries on the life of the country at large – farming innovations certainly sprang from the large monastic holdings – and the activities of some abbots, who ranked among the mightiest landowners.

In this book, I can only try to share my particular interest with you, and that is in the way the different buildings were designed and laid out in order to meet the needs of the monastery. I don't care, therefore, whether the moulding of the window frame reveals a date not later than 1320, although, as I've already said, I happen to prefer it if it is before 1300, but I do greatly care whether the chapter house has a vestibule, or whether the refectory is at right angles to the cloister. I particularly like to see how each abbey has solved the problem of the night stair, the dormitory and the chapter house, and I find the variations in the monks' washing arrangements especially interesting. There are lots of other fascinating items, however, and it is my aim to point you towards them by showing you some of the most outstanding examples of each building or room, and later by listing some of the abbeys I have found more enjoyable with a note of their special features. Some may have lots, others only one. I hope you will be able to add lists of your own favourites.

The Abbey as a Whole

ost abbeys conform to a more or less standard pattern, at least as far as the basic buildings go. The ancillary buildings have many more variables built into their arrangement, while the different types of monastic establishment need different accommodation, and therefore produce slightly different groupings. I repeat, however, that the basic pattern is fairly consistent and, once you have identified one salient feature of the ruins, you should be able to find many of the others.

There is only one major variant which needs to be carefully checked: whether the cloister is south of the church (usual) or north of it (unusual). Unless otherwise specified, by the way, I shall always use points of the compass in a liturgical sense, not a geographical one. East, in other words, is where the high altar is, and the nave ends at the west front.

The plan opposite shows a typical layout, and if you could hold the page up to the light – or to a mirror – you would see an equally typical arrangement of a cloister to the north of the church.

The reason for having the cloister to the south is fairly obvious: the high wall of the church afforded a very useful windbreak and must have made the cloister marginally more bearable on a cold winter's day in the north of England. Only awkward sites would occasionally force the monks to place the cloister to the north. Sometimes the lie of the river (there's always a river) would bring this about, because it's better to have the flow run from the kitchen to the lavatories rather than the other way about.

The plan shown is so self-explanatory that it hardly needs any words, but here are a few. The east range contains the formal day-time rooms, with the dormitory at first floor level, and the reredorter (or lavatory) is usually part of, or attached to, this block. The south range holds the cooking and eating areas, of which the former is sometimes common to the west

The organist's house at Winchester.
I forget what this was, part of the west range perhaps, but it is now a delightful living room.

A typical abbey plan (if it's not Cistercian).

range, which housed the lay brothers – in those orders which had lay brothers – or store rooms and the like. It was closest to the outside world and therefore often had a little office in which dealings with those outside could be conveniently carried on.

The abbot's lodging and the infirmary are not shown on the plan because they were usually outside the main claustral group, and many monasteries had quite a number of secular buildings, such as barns, mills, granaries, guest houses and the like which are also well beyond the immediate confines of the abbey. Many of those have now completely disappeared, or been so radically converted that their former use can hardly even be guessed at, but I hope I shall be able to point you towards one or two examples worth looking at.

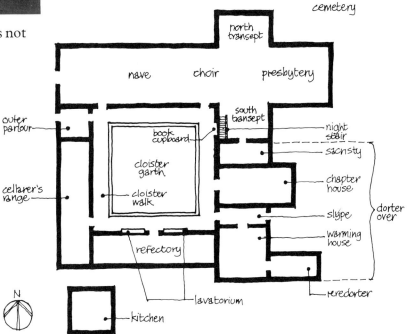

The Abbey Church

The nave at Tewkesbury.
A typical monastic church interior today: chairs; flowers; hymn board, etc. Better than many, however.

Above right: the church at Brinkburn.
A small church, with no significant monastic remains; this is more important for its interior.

Left: the nave at Brinkburn.
Stripped of all but a few choir stalls (though a massive sculpture and an organ lurk in the transepts) this photograph gives some idea of what a monastic church interior might have looked like.

Durham Cathedral is the finest building in the western world.

As I don't approve of forcing my value judgements down other people's throats, I do not put this statement before you as my opinion, but as the considered view of about two dozen leading architectural critics and aesthetes who were asked to nominate their choice. They were quite right, of course. The late and much-lamented Alec Clifton-Taylor said, in his television programme about Durham, that all that many people saw of the Cathedral was the view from the train. And that, he added, was pretty magnificent. Durham Cathedral is an abbey church. If you want to see monastic building at its finest, it is therefore obvious where you must go.

Unfortunately, however, you won't really get much impression of what an abbey church looked like in its heyday by looking at any modern cathedral, even Durham. Don't forget that even the oldest group of buildings only remained in use for about four hundred and fifty years, and that nearly as many years have now passed since the Dissolution of the Monasteries, During these latter four hundred and fifty years many changes and additions have taken place, most of them making it much harder to imagine what the church would have been like when the monks were using it.

I must repeat that, on the whole, I think ruins are more evocative than whole buildings, with only one exception that I can think of in England, and that is Brinkburn Priory, which is complete, but empty and disused. It is a pity, therefore, that it's a rather small building. I really intend only to talk about British sites, but it's probably worth mentioning some foreign examples in case you happen to be passing: Silvacane and Senanque, close to each other in Provence, are excellent examples of whole churches which can be seen empty of trappings.

Let us assume, then, that for one reason or another, you will probably look at the great churches which survive in active use. You will be able to appreciate the architecture, of course, and some of the items of church furniture which tend not to survive in ruins: fonts, for example – there's a lovely font in Winchester Cathedral. Then there are misericords, which have concealed points of interest. As such a large part of the monks' time was spent standing up singing services, they were provided with a very helpful tip-up seat, which gave them a sort of ledge on which to prop themselves in a standing position. What makes these seats interesting is that underneath the ledge, and therefore presumably only visible to the monk if he had eyes in the back of his legs, the woodcarver often placed delightfully comic cameos, or simply beautiful carvings. A school of these carvers were responsible for a whole group of misericords in the north.

Tombs of early abbots can often be found (as well as those of less important dignitaries: kings and things). Sometimes these tombs are housed in chantry chapels, miniature churches within a church, where masses would be sung for the soul of the departed, daily, weekly or annually according to how much money he had bequeathed for the purpose.

It's hardly necessary to list the great churches of

The font at Winchester. *Carved in black marble, this twelfth-century font shows scenes from the life of St Nicholas.*

Above right: the Percy chantry at Tynemouth.
Built in the fifteenth century, such churches within a church were often endowed by rich men with a view to saving their souls.

England where all these delights can be found: there are lots of books which deal with them specifically, but apart from Durham, others which spring readily to my mind are Winchester, Gloucester, Worcester, Tewkesbury, Canterbury and Westminster. Not all great churches are cathedrals; not all cathedrals were monastic; not all monasteries were abbeys. Let us deal with this last point first. I use the words abbey and monastery more or less interchangeably, and I have not attempted to differentiate between abbeys and priories. Generally speaking, abbeys were self-governing, while priories were dependent upon some other establishment; monasteries were for monks, while convents and nunneries were for nuns; friaries were for friars. The difference mattered a lot at the time, but it doesn't matter so much in looking at ruins. The Knights Hospitaller and Templar were two different kinds of military monk, and I haven't dealt with them in any detail, though they get mentioned occasionally. As well as Denny and Ansty, which are in the *Gazetteer*, look out for the Templars' round churches in The Temple (London), Northampton and Cambridge. St Paul's Cathedral and the two Liverpool Cathedrals are obvious non-monastic examples of their genre, and I'm sure there are others, even of monastic date. Some parish churches are as large as some cathedrals, but were built as such and not as part of a monastery.

Finally, there were a number of near-monastic foundations known as minsters, to which a college of priests might be attached, but following no monastic rule. Many great churches of this type survive, but I'm not dealing with them in this book, so I'll just throw in a passing reference to Beverley, Wimborne, Wells and Lincoln.

As a sort of half-way house on the way towards ruins, I ought to deal with partial ruins. The reason why these exist is very interesting. When monasteries were founded, they were usually sited in remote places, far from towns and villages. Soon, though, little settlements tended to develop around them, especially when lay people were employed to carry out some of the work on the farms and fisheries of the abbey. Naturally, these people wanted somewhere to worship, and so they were allowed to attend services in the nave of the church, although they would have been cut off by a formidable screen from the monks in the choir. When the abbeys were dissolved, these communities were left without a parish church, and so they some-

The nave at Waltham Abbey. *Durham in miniature. Beyond the present east end, now marked by a wall of vastly inferior architecture, lay the choir and the grave of King Harold.*

times bought the nave from the King or the person to whom he had sold the monastery, and the rest of the church was pulled down. Worksop is one such church; Waltham Abbey is another, and in the latter case the effect of pulling down the choir of the church has been to place the grave of King Harold, which was naturally next to the High Altar, in the open air. (A brief aside on the subject of Harold: everyone knows that he lost the battle of Hastings; not everyone knows that he had won a terrific victory in the north-east only a fortnight before, and had succeeded in marching his not very disciplined army south in order to

The south porch at Malmesbury.
Protected from the elements, this sculpture is in better condition than most. It dates from the twelfth century.

The watching loft at St Bartholomew's.
A room projecting into the presbytery enabled a monk to keep a discreet watch on the high altar. You may just be able to make out Prior Bolton's rebus on the front.

meet the new threat from William of Normandy.) Malmesbury was chopped off at both ends, but still retains some beautiful features: the south doorway has some remarkable stone carving, while what remains of the nave is handsome Norman work. All the east end has gone, however, and most of the first two bays of the west end. Cistercians never had lay people in their churches, which is why fewer of their churches got turned over to parish use.

In only one case that I know of, Boxgrove Priory, the congregation obviously decided that they preferred the monks' part of the church to their own, and so they bought the choir, leaving the nave to be pulled down. I have to make an appalling admission: soon after I had written this paragraph, I realised that the church I can actually see from my office is another example – St Bartholomew's.

I like ruins, however, and I think that many churches look even better half demolished. When you can see the arcades of the choir at Rievaulx or the nave at Buildwas without any enclosing walls, you can appreciate them even more. But even when such architectural treats are denied you, there are still lots of interesting things to look for on the site of the abbey church: altars and side chapels, for example. As more and more monks became fully professed priests, they each had to say mass every day and one

Above right: the crossing at Boxgrove.
Here you see the site of the demolished nave, with its north arcade blocked to form a wall.

Right: the nave at Buildwas.
As at Rievaulx, the loss of the outer walls enables one better to appreciate the structure.

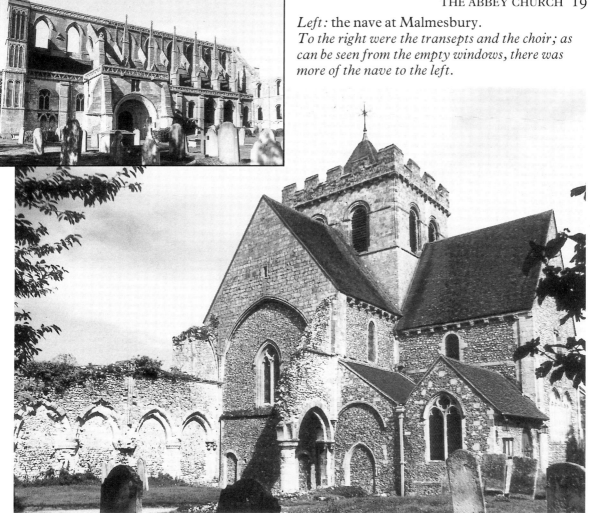

Left: the nave at Malmesbury.
To the right were the transepts and the choir; as can be seen from the empty windows, there was more of the nave to the left.

The east end at Fountains.
This is a view from the south of the chapel of the nine altars.
The lower doorway led to a passage from the infirmary, and
the upper one to the abbot's private apartments.

The chapel of the nine altars at
Fountains.
Each professed priest had to say
mass every day, and so many
altars were needed to make this
possible.

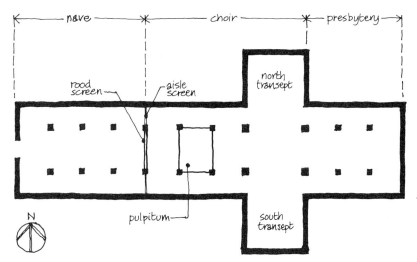

An abbey church plan.

Above: the choir at Rievaulx. *Though the east end remains, the north and south walls have gone, allowing the arcade of the choir to be better appreciated. The ruins of the infirmary and abbot's buildings are in the foreground.*

Left: Roche abbey church. *Photographed on a misty day, this shows the base of the rood screen in the foreground, which separated the monks' church from the lay brothers' nave. There are signs of altars against the screen, the existence of which enabled more priests to say mass at any time.*

altar alone was not enough. Even the chapel of the nine altars at Fountains (and Durham) would have had long queues, if such things had existed in those days. More altars had to be provided, and so little chapels were fitted into the transepts, the side aisles, and even up against the individual pillars of the nave. Traces of even these last can often be found.

Also in the nave of the church, you can find traces of the rood screen and the pulpitum, which made two divisions in the length of the church. The pulpitum was often a double screen, with a platform between, on which the organ was placed and from which sometimes some singing or reading took place. You can see a very good surviving example in Norwich Cathedral. Nowadays we often tend loosely to speak of the choir as being the part of the church east of the crossing, but the pulpitum, marking its western end, was very often set two or three bays into the nave, so that the choir stretched across the transepts. By contrast at Canterbury, where there is another excellent example, the pulpitum is at the eastern side of the crossing, at a higher level.

The rood screen was a simpler affair in some ways, with a crucifix above it and an altar against its west face, of which you can see an excellent ruined example at Tynemouth. It was placed one bay further west than the western part of the pulpitum, so that there was a single bay passageway between the two. The aisles to the side of the rood screen were also closed by screens, so that everything east of that point was cut off for exclusive use by the monks.

Tiled floors can occasionally be seen in ruined churches, whereas in active churches they have often been succeeded by Victorian replicas. Byland is the best place for seeing them *in situ*, but in the parish church of Muchelney, just alongside the abbey ruins, there are some very fine tiles which may have come from the abbey.

The reason you won't always find a west door in an abbey ruin is not that it has disappeared in the decay: it is often because there wasn't one. You didn't need a great processional door for the outside world to come through, since the church existed to serve the monks. Their main doors were the east and west processional doorways into the cloister, plus the night stair where one existed, and so if the site made it at all difficult, as at Buildwas, they didn't bother. At Furness, the entrance for the laity is really peculiar. The west end has been set into ground which rises steeply all round it, and so people had to come down a stairway against the north wall of the church, and enter through a small door a couple of bays eastwards.

Just outside the west front of the church, where west doors do exist, you can often find traces of a low porch, frequently known as a Galilee. Fountains and Rievaulx each clearly had such a narthex, where the monks probably assembled to process into church, but at Durham the Galilee takes the form of a large chapel, a little lower down the hill on which the church stands: there is no west door except from church to chapel.

What really excites me inside the church, however, is the night stair. This is closely connected with the chapter house location, and it's very hard to consider one without the other, but as I have chosen to consider the buildings feature by feature, I'll have to skirt round the problem now, and deal with it in greater

Tiles at Byland.
On the steps of a chapel in the transept, these are among the most extensive remains of their type. A very similar panel can be seen in the British Museum.

Above right: the west door at Portchester.
A simple door for a simple church.

detail when I reach the chapter house itself.

As many of the services took place in the small hours and as, even today, the climate in Yorkshire, for example, is not noted for its balminess, many monastic orders made it possible for the monks to go directly to church (do not pass *Go*, do not collect £200) from the dormitory, by a stairway down into the south transept – or north, from a northern cloister. I don't know why, but to me the image of the monks processing down the night stair into church is one of the most evocative in the whole ensemble.

There is an enormous range of night stairs to be found and, as I've hinted above, their form is partly dictated by the need to get over or round the chapter house. The first thing to look for is an actual stair in the south transept, frequently running along the west wall, and rising to a hole in the south wall at first-floor level. That's the standard form, but the fun lies in seeing the variations.

By far the most imposing night stair I know is in

The night stair at Hexham.
*The grandest in the country, leading to a broad landing over
a slype. The object on the extreme right is a Roman tombstone.*

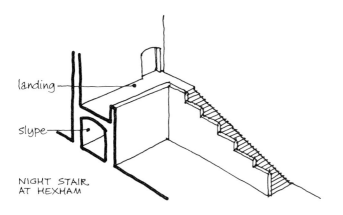

landing —

slype —

NIGHT STAIR
AT HEXHAM

USUAL
NIGHT STAIR

A typical night stair and
Hexham's splendid (untypical)
example.

The night stair at Bristol.
Here the stair runs up within the thickness of the south wall of the transept.

Hexham Abbey. Apart from its grandeur as a night stair, it has at least two other interesting aspects: the treads are filled with lead from the roof burnt down in one of the many border squabbles; and there's a Roman tombstone at the foot of the stairs so fine that a cast of it is to be found in the Museum of Roman Civilisation in Rome itself. The reason for the grandeur is, as far as I know, unique. The broad and easy-going stairway leads up to a landing which is inside the transept, and it sits over a slype (or passageway) which is outside the transept. I've often tried to explain this to people without any great success, so I've had it drawn for you (and me) opposite; perhaps it will be even clearer if I also show the more usual arrangement.

By contrast, as far as I can make out, the night stair at Lindisfarne, on Holy Island, is only an ordinary little circular stair, but then Lindisfarne has a very peculiar layout altogether. Perhaps a better example of the extra-mural night stair (if you see what I mean) is that at Bristol Cathedral, formerly Abbey. Here you go through a small unassuming hole in the wall, at present guarded by a wrought iron gate, and turn right to go up a narrow stair parallel to the south wall. At the top, you do another right-angled turn to the left and you're heading for the dorter (or dormitory).

Very often, the stair was of wood, and so there's nothing at all to be seen, while sometimes you can trace the line of treads and risers on the west wall of the transept. The clue is almost always the presence of a door-sized opening at about first-floor level, and usually near the junction of the south and west walls of the transept. In some cases, the kindly custodians will have put a new wooden stair in, to give you an idea of what it would have been like.

An unusual but not unique variant is to be found at Dryburgh, one of that magnificent quartet of Border Abbeys; Jedburgh, Melrose and Kelso being the other three. There the stair goes on rising through the south transept wall before reaching landing level. (You'll hear more about Dryburgh when we reach chapter houses.) A very peculiar type is at Hailes, where the stair apparently rose within the thickness of the south wall of the transept.

All too often, the hole in the south wall leads nowhere, because not all that many first-floor buildings remain. Durham has a complete dormitory, but it's uncommon. A reversal of this usual pattern is to be found at Cleeve. The church has almost completely disappeared there, but the dormitory survives, so that what you can see is a hole leading from nowhere to somewhere – at least if you're standing in the church which, in this chapter, you are.

It's a pity, really, that night stairs come so early in the natural progression round a monastery, because they're one of my great enthusiasms, and I could go on about them for a long time. However, I suppose I had better move on to other matters, and leave you to look for excitingly idiosyncratic exits of your own. Should I mention the lay brothers' night stair at this juncture? Perhaps not, so I'll leave it till we get right round the cloister and come back to the west end of the church. If I've succeeded in arousing some enthusiasm in you about night stairs, you can have that to look forward to while we're dealing with less exciting thinks like slypes.

Of course, for those who delight in studying the development of architectural styles, the church is the best place to see it, and in far too many cases the church is the only standing element of any consequence. Increasing familiarity will lead you to see all sorts of interesting variations: aisle-less churches; one-aisled churches; or the most elaborate complexes. As abbeys grew to be centres of pilgrimages, frequently to see the holy relics assiduously assembled there, the need grew for an effective one-way system past the shrines. Choirs were rebuilt in extended form, often with a

The night stair at Kirkstall. *Just through the doorway, on your right, is the treasury.*

Above: the south transept of
Dryburgh.
*The night stair rises in two stages
through the south wall; the east
processional doorway leads down
to the cloister; the small dark
doorway leads to the vestry.*

Right: the night stair at Melrose.
*When the cloister is on the north,
the night stair, or the doorway in
the wall, will usually be on the left
hand side of the north transept.
You can see where the stairway
was, by the unfinished stonework.*

series of small chapels, although the chevet form – a ring of radiating chapels all the way round the curve of the east end – is not so familiar in England as on the continent. One of the best examples of a chevet, at Croxden, has a main road running through the middle of it. This makes following in the pilgrims' footsteps a bit hazardous, but it's well worth a look (and both ways before crossing the road).

Mediaeval rebuilders were not so conservation-conscious as many are today, and there are often curious clashes of style where elements of different dates meet. For example, at Bolton Abbey (strictly speaking, a priory) a tower has been just slapped up against the west front. Sometimes there are even slight changes of direction – Canterbury Cathedral is a famous example – so that the choir and the nave meet at an angle. Very often, however, these dramatic changes seem to work together quite happily – and there may be a message there.

We will now leave the church by the east processional doorway into the cloister.

Above: the chevet at Hailes.
You can clearly see the pattern of radiating chapels around the east end of the church.

Above right: the nave at Croxden.
Looking through the west door, you can see my car parked on the road which runs through the nave from south east to north west.

Right: east processional doorway at Byland.
A succession of curved steps leads down from the nave to the cloister level, thus easing the circulation problems posed by the night stair and the chapter house.

The Cloister

The cloister is the hub of the monastic wheel. Around it circles and from it radiates all the remainder of the abbey life. Indeed, 'the cloister' is often used as a synonym for the abbey. There are really three parts to the cloister: the buildings around it; the garth (or garden) within it; and the cloister walk itself. We can dismiss the first from this chapter, since the buildings will get plenty of individual attention. There are very few points of great interest to be found within the garden, but they are worth some notice.

At Worcester, an attempt has been made to recreate the kind of herb garden which might have been found in the abbey's lifetime (and I hear that they are going to do the same at Castle Acre), although no doubt in many monasteries the infirmarer or an assistant may have had his herbarium nearer at hand to the scene of his ministrations. In Gloucester and Wenlock, the interest lies in the way in which the lavatorium creeps into the inner garth, disturbing its usual regularity. In many places, you may find tombs of more important persons, though the monks' cemetery was usually elsewhere.

Apart from the special case of the Carthusians, the cloister was much of a muchness in most abbeys, usually being around 100 or 120 feet square. Finchale was as small as 75 feet, while Rievaulx was as large as 140 feet square, and I can't be sure that those represent the extremes. The whole of the garth was surrounded by a covered walk, of which the north walk directly abutted the south wall of either the nave or the south aisle of the church.

In that north walk can sometimes be found – certainly at Cleeve – the decorative stonework marking the site of the collation seat, the place for the abbot's chair where he sat while readings were made from the *Collationes Patrum*, an improving work; and at Strata Florida, which I haven't seen, I believe that

Right: the cloister at Cleeve. *The upper floor to the left is the dormitory, and the large windows to the right light the fifteenth-century refectory in the south range. The doorways, left to right, are: library; chapter house; day stair; parlour; two slypes; two small rooms (then the lavatorium) and the stair to the refectory.*

Below: the cloister at Worcester. *It isn't easy for the amateur to get aerial views, but this is taken from the church tower. You can see almost the whole cloister walk; the great chapter house is on the left; and the refectory runs across the top of the photo. The herb garden is in shadow just to the right of the sunlit bush.*

Below right: the cloister at Fountains.
The north east corner, showing (from left to right) the
east processional doorway, the blocked book cupboard,
the library, and the triple entrance to the chapter house.

The east cloister walk at Lacock.
The entrance to the chapter house is on the right, and the doorway to the warming house is beyond it.

you can see the site of the lectern from which the reading was done. As we shall see in dealing with the library, abbeys were heavily dependent upon copying for the acquisition of new books, and there had to be somewhere for that copying to be done. Since there are very few examples in England of rooms specially built or set aside for that purpose, the north walk also doubled as the scriptorium in many abbeys. Of course, many cloisters must have been horribly draughty, since they often consisted of open arcades onto the central garth, but at Gloucester there are stone carrels with small window openings, which must have made much more congenial studies, in which the work of writing or copying could be carried on. In a few public schools small half-partitioned studies are still called carrels, and I am told that the same is true in American universities and many libraries.

As I have just said, the cloister was often open to the weather, but others – or the same ones later – had dwarf walls between the columns, and the smaller the openings above no doubt the pleasanter it was in

The north cloister walk at Gloucester.
Observe the cubicles on the left. These would have been extended by wooden partitions to form carrels, for individual monks to read and write in.

The cloister at Lacock.
From this view you would never guess that you were looking at an elegant stately home.

The east cloister walk at Bristol.
A simple sloping timber roof.

winter. The roof of the cloister usually sloped down from the walls of the buildings around it, so that rainwater was naturally shed into the centre, but while some were simply pitched roofs carried on rafters, others were quite elaborately vaulted underneath. Gloucester has a very fine stone vault, as does Worcester, while Bristol has the simple timber roof.

The form of the colonnade followed fairly closely the architectural style of the building period, so that the earliest have simple Norman round arches, and the later ones can have quite elaborate tracery, resembling the windows of the church they adjoin. Sometimes the cloister walk can be a thing of beauty in itself, and even the fragment at Muchelney (where, incidentally, the upper floor sat over the cloister walk itself in an unusual manner) contains very fine vaulting; but even where only a few stone fragments remain, the outline of the cloister can usually be discerned and is the key to tracing many of the other component parts of the monastery.

Some Slypes

 lypes are simply passages and, in our context, usually through the ring of claustral buildings – claustral is simply the adjective from cloister – to the outer reaches of the monastery. There is almost always one leading to the infirmary, and this is usually placed near the south-east corner of the cloister, passing through the eastern range.

It's not unusual for there to be two passages through the eastern arm of the cloister, since frequently there was a slype immediately abutting the south transept – in fact that's about all that remains of the claustral buildings at Whitby. The reason for these north-eastern passages is not always clear: they don't seem to lead anywhere in particular, and at Fountains for example, it merely gives access to a yard enclosed by the eastern arm of the church, the south transept, the chapter house, and another passage leading to the chapel of the nine altars.

Sometimes, it seems fairly clear, they doubled as book cupboards or even sacristies, and it just happened that you could get in at one end and out at the other. Nowadays, they can hardly be said to be one of the most enthralling parts of monastic remains, but Cleeve and Battle, to name but two, both have rather nicely roofed examples, with a stony floor, which can look quite dramatic when the sun is in the right direction. They can also provide good frames for photographs – and sometimes they can even help you to get from one part of the abbey to another.

A slype at Cleeve.
A passageway through the south range.

Libraries and Book Cupboards

ometimes one, sometimes the other, and sometimes even both are to be found in nearly every monastic ruin. It seems to me that the reason why both existed side by side is that one was short term and the other was long term. You borrowed a book from the library, but at the end of the day's reading session you put it in the book cupboard until the next day. Books were not the abundant commodity in the Middle Ages which they are today, when probably every one of my readers owns more books than most monasteries did – always excepting the sort of library featured in the vastly overpraised *Name of the Rose*. I own several thousand books, and a friend of mine had 14,000 at the last count. I reckon that most monasteries had only 100 or so books before the invention of printing, although the greater foundations gradually acquired surprisingly large collections: Canterbury had about 4,000 at the Dissolution. They obtained new books either as gifts or by copying examples lent to them by other abbeys.

These precious objects were therefore kept in a safe place, usually immediately adjoining the south transept. There is almost always some small room interposed between the transept and the chapter house (although not at Monk Bretton or Tynemouth) and this was either a slype between the cloister and the cemetery, for example, or else a small room which might be a sacristy (the function of which you will find described more fully in the chapter on *Various Other Rooms*), a library, or both. In this latter case, the library would adjoin the cloister, and the sacristy would be the eastern half of the room, perhaps with direct access to the church. I'm sorry there are so many either/ors and perhapses in this section: unfortunately, you can't avoid them hereabouts.

You can usually tell fairly easily when the area was a passage rather than a room or rooms. It's usually narrow, and has obvious doors at both ends. At Whitby,

Right: the east range at Furness.
The row of multi-ordered doorways: book cupboard; chapter house; book cupboard; parlour; slype. The narrow windows above lit the dormitory.

Below: a book cupboard at Furness.
The dark little space behind, about ten feet square, is belied by the magnificent doorway.

it slopes so steeply that it couldn't have been anything else. When it appears to have been a room, you can sometimes clearly see the division into two, and occasionally you can even see signs of shelving, which helps to identify the library. Unusually, at Cleeve the library is south of the sacristy, both run the full depth of the east range, and there is no sign of a book cupboard.

Signs of shelving are more easily found in the book cupboards, which are usually set into the thickness of the south transept wall. You can trace the grooves into which the shelves were slotted and doubtless there were also wooden doors to the cupboard.

In one case I know of there is a very strange and interesting variation. In the chapter on the chapter house (and that awkward use of English is a clue to something else you'll read there) you will be told that the entrance to it is almost invariably three-fold: usually a grand central door, with two slightly less grand side doors or windows. That is what appears to be the case at Furness, but really the two side entrances are both book cupboards, flanking the central entrance which therefore becomes a short passageway into the chapter house proper. These book cupboards are so capacious that the two together are probably as big as many another abbey's library.

The Chapter House

We come now to the second part of the night stair/dormitory problem. The chapter house was a very important room in the monastic complex, second only to the church, even though the refectory was usually bigger. The reason for its importance is that all the serious business of the abbey was transacted there, including the notices of forthcoming events, the publication of duty rosters, the administration of punishments, and one other item. Not many people know why it was called the chapter house – perhaps they have never even asked themselves why. It is because a chapter of the rule by which the monks lived was read there (every day, in the case of Cistercians) to the assembled body. The place where the chapter was read became the 'chapter' house, and the body meeting there later became 'The Chapter', as in 'The Dean and Chapter'. Thus, the name for a part of a book became the name for a body of men. At Byland, in the museum, survive the remnants of a lectern from which the chapter was read.

At any rate, you can now see why the chapter house was so important. It couldn't therefore be a poky little room, and yet it had to form part of a range of not very important buildings. The obvious answer is to have it stick up a bit. But if you do that, it gets in the way of the dormitory, which runs from the south transept straight over the chapter house. Split-level dorters were not in vogue in twelfth-century England.

Two basic solutions were adopted: either the chapter house was excavated a little, so that you went down to get into it; or a vestibule was formed, over which the dormitory ran, and the chapter house then stuck out behind, and stuck up at the same time. Don't be misled by Wells: although it is one of the finest chapter houses, and certainly has what I regard as the most magnificent approach, it was not monastic, and therefore didn't have the dormitory problem to

The chapter house lectern at Byland.
The wooden part is a reconstruction, but most of the base is original. From such a lectern a 'chapter', giving the room its name, was read every day.

Above: the east cloister walk at Boxgrove.
One of the few churches where the parish bought the choir. The cloister was on the north side, and the picture shows the typical tripartite chapter house doorway and windows, with the north transept and the (blocked) east processional doorway.

Left: The chapter house stair at Wells.
Do not be deceived. This is magnificent, but it's not monastic.

worry about. Wells is a minster, like Southwell and Beverley, but they're all well worth a visit for other reasons than abbatial ones.

It is when you look at the individual versions of these two systems that you begin to get the variations that I find so interesting. The first method is very often coupled with a slight descent from the church into the cloister; at Byland it's about seven elegant semi-circular steps. Immediately, therefore, the amount by which the night stair has to climb to reach first floor level has been reduced by a few feet. True, this does nothing to make the chapter house taller than the library or the parlour, but at least it makes the vestibule – if there is one – more high and grand without pushing the dormitory too far up the transept wall.

At Lacock, you go down a mere couple of steps from the cloister, but at Buildwas, where the cloister is already well below the level of the church, you go down five steps to get to chapter house floor level. At Dryburgh, where we've already noted the curious behaviour of the night stair, the cloister is about five steps down through the east processional doorway, and the chapter house floor is a further five feet or so down. This is the deepest descent I can think of, offhand. However deep or shallow the excavated type of chapter house, it only partially succeeds, I think, in its aim of producing a grand conference room. The

Above: the chapter house at Buildwas.
As you can see, my wife – a tall woman – is sunk to the waist by the excavated floor, which allowed the dormitory to pass uninterrupted over the top.

Above left: the chapter house at Buildwas.
Viewed from inside, the difference in level of the cloister is easily seen. It was therefore easy for the dormitory to run straight overhead.

Dryburgh's solution to running the dorter over the chapter house.

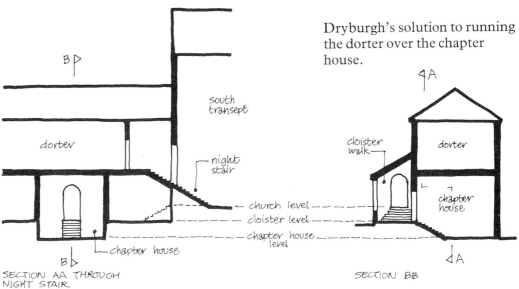

SECTION AA THROUGH NIGHT STAIR

SECTION BB

Above: the chapter house at Bristol.
This photograph is an attempt to show how the chapter house rises above and behind the main east range, in which the dorter only begins south of the chapter house (the first floor windows on the left), being reached by a passage over a vestibule.

Left: the chapter house at Bristol.
This soaring room could never have been possible if the dormitory had had to pass over it.

semi-subterranean effect is not only a bit gloomy, but also it tends to dampness.

Type two (or three, if you count those which never attempt the grandiose, and confine themselves within the natural limits of the ground floor) produces more, and sometimes more exciting, variations. In some cases the vestibule is only part of the width of the dormitory, so that there is a passage over the vestibule and past the upper part of the chapter house before the dorter proper begins. Bristol is an excellent example of this type. In quite a few others, the vestibule is the full width of the dormitory, so that the full height of the chapter house is only achieved after a very sizeable anteroom. Kirkstall is like this: the two parts are almost equally large, and the same is true at Bayham.

Bristol's solution: a vestibule.

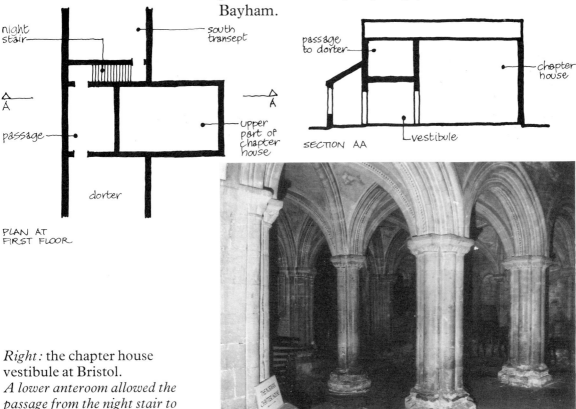

night stair

south transept

passage

upper part of chapter house

dorter

PLAN AT FIRST FLOOR

passage to dorter

chapter house

SECTION AA

vestibule

Right: the chapter house vestibule at Bristol.
A lower anteroom allowed the passage from the night stair to reach the dormitory.

Sometimes there is no vestibule as such, but the chapter house appears to have been one room with two heights. Presumably the abbot and senior officers of the monastery sat in the higher bit, while the rank and file monks sat in the low headroom. At Cleeve there is a very strange version of this type, in that the part which projects out and up is only half as long as the part beneath the dormitory: this must have produced a very strange effect when still standing, but only the lower part remains now.

One easy way out is to have the chapter house outside the eastern range altogether, and probably the most famous example of this is Westminster, where the building adjoins the cloister on two of its eight sides only, and is approached by a vestibule consisting of little more than a passageway.

The simplest method of coping with the dorter is, of course, to keep your room within the constraints imposed. Perhaps have a couple of steps down, and of course keep the cloister below church level if possible, but then your room will have to be fairly modest in its proportions.

Above: the east side of the chapter house at Cleeve.
The low vestibule below the dormitory soared up to a short higher section, now demolished, beyond the east range. The effect must have been very strange.

Above right: the chapter house at Worcester.
This shape is more likely to be found in Benedictine than Cistercian monasteries.

The curious case of Cleeve and (*opposite*) the more usual case of Bayham.

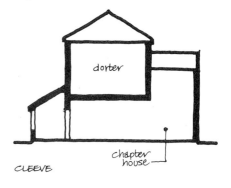

CLEEVE

Right: the chapter house at Hailes.

A typical square-ended Cistercian room, with two rows of columns and a Trinity entrance: the central door flanked by windows.

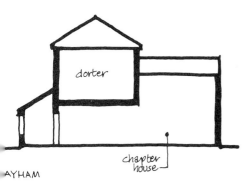

AYHAM

The Norman arcading of Wenlock's chapter house.
The full height of the chapter house throughout its depth is possible because there was no night stair connection to the dormitory.

The chapter house at Kirkstall.
Without steps to avoid the clash of dormitory and chapter house, the latter was often low for its length and breadth.

Apart from the extra-mural types of chapter house, most, whether soaring behind the dorter or not, are square-ended, although Rievaulx is a notable exception, terminating in an apsidal end which contained an ambulatory outside the inner wall of the chapter house itself. The proportions are usually much the same in length and breadth, whether they had a central row of columns, two rows, or none at all: about 2:1. At Sawley, however, it is about 3:1.

I've gone on at considerable length about these variations because I find them one of the most interesting facets of abbey exploration. There are lots of other fascinating aspects to be observed as well, such as the decoration on the walls or the layout and form of any columns. Perhaps you will seek out the remnants of the monks' seating, but there's sure to be something for everyone in the chapter house.

Top right: the chapter house doorway at Kirkstall.
When there weren't three openings, there were six – very occasionally: twin doors, with two windows on either side.

Centre right: the chapter house at Rievaulx.
You can see the rounded east end, and some of the tombs in the floor.

Lower right: the chapter house at Rievaulx.
Viewed from the other end, this shows the inner wall of the ambulatory, and the grass in the foreground was part of the walkway. The stone benches around the side can be clearly seen.

The Warming House

In most abbeys, the warming house (or cale-factorium) tended to be in the east range, just about at the point where it reached the end of the cloister and passed the south range. In Cistercian abbeys, it is almost invariably to be found in the south range itself, abutting the south-east corner, using the space realised by the turning round of the refectory to be at right angles to the range.

I know that the Cistercians aimed at greater austerity than some other orders, but it has always struck me as an unnecessary piece of austerity to move the warming house out from underneath the dormitory. Perhaps there was too much competition for the beds over the warming house, and it was felt by the powers that were that the move would make everyone equally cold.

In the chapter on kitchens you will be warned against being misled into thinking that every fireplace tells a story: it's also true here. Very often there are lots of fireplaces in the ground floor of the eastern range, but look for the brick. On the whole, brick represents a post-suppression insertion. Sometimes, just to confuse matters still further, you will find brick improvements of monastic fireplaces in rooms which really were warming houses.

Apart from the Cistercian siting, of which Fountains is a splendid example, the warming house tended to be one or two rooms further south than the chapter house, in the eastern range. Sometimes the parlour would intervene, and sometimes it seems to have formed part of an indeterminate undercroft, also possibly used as the novices' room. Occasionally, there may even have been *two* fireplaces, one in the warming house and the other in the novices' room.

I have not been able to discover for what proportion of the year a fire was lit, and of course it was only for a very limited part of the day that the monk will have been permitted to warm himself, but I think we can

The warming house at Fountains.
This was the easternmost room in the south range. You can see one of the two great fireplaces, and we can assume that the supporting timbers are modern.

The warming house at Lacock.
I forget what the cauldron was for,
but the nuns of Lacock probably
had a good use for it.

safely assume that getting comfortably stuffy in a warm, draught-free room was not a significant feature of monastic life. I imagine that monks who were working at copying manuscripts, or even composing original works, may have been allowed more frequent recourse to the fire to keep their fingers supple.

Just because you can't find a fireplace at all does not mean that a particular monastery lacked a calefactorium altogether. In some early buildings or smaller establishments the fire was provided as in a mediaeval hall: on a central hearth or in a brazier, and the smoke made its way out through the roof, windows, or a special vent. Anyway, if you think that wherever you are staying while looking at monasteries could be a bit more comfortable, spare a thought for the monks, who would have been up since before dawn, as they snatched a brief respite by the fire.

The Refectory

The frater was second only to the church in size – although the lay brothers' range at Fountains was much longer, and the volume of the infirmary hall if considered as a whole was certainly much greater. As a rule, however, this generalisation is true. It is also true that as a rule there was only one main meal a day, although in some orders a second meal was served in the summer. Don't forget that life was much more affected then by the hours of daylight and darkness, so that the working day was actually longer in summer.

Once again, I have a favourite item to look out for in the refectory: it is the wall pulpit. Eating, like just about everything else, was not the occasion for idle gossip. The monks ate discreetly and silently, while a chosen brother stood in the pulpit, reading from improving works such as the Gospels, the lives of the fathers, or learned commentaries. Finding these pulpits today is not always easy, because they were usually formed within the thickness of the wall, thus weakening it, so that if there has been any tendency to fall down in the area of the refectory, this is where it is most likely to manifest itself.

Several splendid and complete examples remain, and many interesting traces in addition. At Tintern only the doorway remains, while at Rievaulx you can clearly see where the stair and the pulpit formerly were. By contrast, at Shrewsbury (home of the fictional monk detective, Cadfael) the pulpit stands alone in a rather ill-kept garden, across the main road which runs past the church. At Worcester there is a curious case of an entrance from the south cloister walk into the pulpit stair, so that the reader must have emerged somewhat to the surprise of his audience, rather like Mr Punch. Chester has a very fine complete example, but probably the best of all is at Beaulieu. Most people go to Beaulieu for the cars – and so do I – and the monastic remains are not, on the whole, very

Below: the refectory pulpit at Fountains.
The doorway admits to the staircase, and the visitor can walk up to address some words – improving, one hopes – to his friends.

Right: the refectory at Chester.
At the end, behind the dais, is the doorway leading to the wall pulpit. You can see the line of the rising staircase on the right.

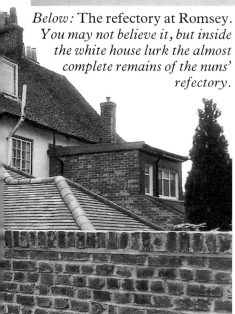

Below: The refectory at Romsey. *You may not believe it, but inside the white house lurk the almost complete remains of the nuns' refectory.*

thrilling; but the refectory is exceptional. I expect that, at this point, anyone who has been to Beaulieu for the cars and had a quick look round will say: 'Refectory? What refectory?' The answer is: the parish church. The frater was converted into the church, and therefore not only has the building remained remarkably intact, but the pulpit has also remained to fulfil its function.

Refectories do rather lend themselves to conversion, and they sometimes turn up in odd places. It has recently been discovered that the only substantial monastic remains at Romsey (which was a nunnery and is, incidentally, well worth a visit for the church alone) lie hidden within a very ordinary-looking white-painted house just to the south of the abbey grounds. Apparently, virtually the whole refectory is still there, though well concealed by the later domestic adaptation.

The new refectory at Cleeve. *The dais for the abbot is at the far end, and on the right, beyond the modern (sixteenth century) fireplace is the doorway to the refectory pulpit.*

Originally, nearly all refectories formed most of the south range; very often they will have been raised above an undercroft and traces of steps can sometimes be found, as at Bayham; or perhaps the lower storey will itself only remain in vestigial form as at Jedburgh. Gradually, in the Cistercian order, the growth in numbers of both sorts of monk made more complicated kitchen arrangements desirable, and you couldn't then accommodate all the clerical monks parallel to the cloister. The frater was therefore rebuilt at right angles to the centre of the south cloister walk. This, as it happened, released space for the warming house at the eastern end of the range, and also made possible the provision of a sizable kitchen between the refectory and the lay brothers' range to the west. For the amateur monastic ruin visitor, then, a very quick and easy way of displaying expertise is to note whether the frater is parallel or at right angles and to say: 'Well, this obviously is (or isn't) a Cistercian abbey.' You'll go wrong, however, at Cleeve.

Cleeve is a special case for more than one reason. It was built late enough for its original refectory to be at right angles, but by the late fifteenth century numbers had declined, particularly of lay brothers, and the frater was rebuilt parallel to the cloister. The result is a hall from the last period of monastic life, with an outstanding timber roof. Traces of the pulpit steps remain, but the pulpit itself was destroyed by the insertion of a post-Dissolution fireplace. An even more exciting consequence of the rebuild, however, was that the floor of the thirteenth-century frater was simply covered over where it now projected behind the later model. When this was exposed in modern times, it revealed what may not, if you believe Winchester, be the largest area of mediaeval tiling to be seen in the country, but may well be the best-preserved large area. It may still be covered in winter, so make sure your visit is in the summer.

GROUND FLOOR

Galilee or narthex —
church
cellarage —
cloister garth
cloister walk
lay brothers' dorter over
outer parlour —
lay brothers' refectory —
N
kitchen —
refectory —
warming house —
night stair
library
sacristy
chapter house
parlour
slype
day stair
novices' room

FIRST FLOOR

dorter
upper part of chapter house
reredorter

Below: Cleeve's new refectory. *Rebuilt – behind the large first floor windows – parallel to the cloister, leaving the floor of the old one jutting out.*

Above: a typical Cistercian plan, with refectory at right angles to the cloister.

Below: Cleeve's old refectory. *The mediaeval tiles, now revealed, were simply covered with earth.*

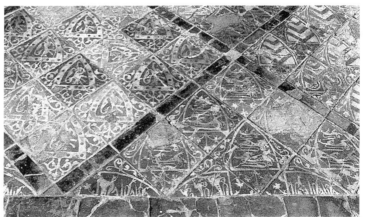

There are a few other interesting sidelines to be looked for, apart from lavatoria and towel cupboards which are dealt with elsewhere. There are other kinds of cupboard to be found, frequently just inside the doorway. At Hailes there are two basins and four cupboards, three of them with grooves for shelves, all in the northern wall, which may have held cutlery and the like. A final domestic touch often to be seen, of which there is a good example at Monk Bretton, is the serving hatch from the kitchen.

The Lavatorium

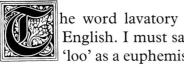he word lavatory has a curious history in English. I must say that I much prefer it to 'loo' as a euphemism for water closet. However, it originally meant a place to wash, and the lavatorium is not to be confused with the reredorter (latrine) or the garderobe (individual closet – except at Hailes, where there's a back to back pair). It is the place where the monks washed their hands before

The lavatorium at Wenlock.
This shows how the wash place was sited inside the cloister garden. The topiary marking the west walk is not monastic. Inset: *the twelfth-century carving.*

entering the refectory, and is almost always therefore to be found in the immediate vicinity of the frater doorway.

The usual pattern is fairly standard, but there are (at least) two glorious exceptions. I'll keep you waiting for those while we deal with the normal type. The most common sort is a recess in the wall of the south range, with an arch or two formed above it, and sometimes with some sort of wall decoration or arcading. At a convenient height would be a stone ledge on which a lead basin would have stood. A supply of water would have been brought to this, often piped, and the holes for the taps can sometimes be seen above the ledge. The used water was almost invariably led away to the main drain from below the basin, and at Hailes there even seems to have been some kind of inspection hatch to the waste channel. A towel would have been provided, and towel cupboards can sometimes be found – I think that the elaborate cupboard in the fragmentary remains of the Muchelney cloister is one such. Extensive examples of the standard type can be seen at Rievaulx and at Fountains, where the lavatorium stretches some way on both sides of the frater doorway. At Norwich, there is a very decorative two-arched wash place which, unusually, is in the wall of the western range.

On the continent, it is not so rare as in Britain – the climate again – but very occasionally here the lavatorium was not in the cloister walk but inside the cloister garth. Doubtless it was not in the open, as it might have been further south, but was housed in a little sort of gazebo. What makes the lavatorium at Wenlock so interesting is not just its position in the south-west corner of the cloister garth, but also the fact that it has fine late twelfth-century carvings on the sides of the washing trough. Bare foundations remain of a similarly positioned example at St Augustine's.

If you want to see the finest washing place in any monastery – or possibly anywhere – you must go to Gloucester Cathedral. There, the lavatorium is on the inside of the south cloister walk, rather than the outside, and projects into the garth. The fan vaulting which roofs it is as fine as anything to be seen in Westminster or Sherborne; the stone trough and drainholes are well preserved; and the whole washing area is like a chapel in miniature. There is also a splendid towel cupboard opposite, where you might usually expect to find the lavatorium itself. Even I, who have always thought that a little honest dirt never did food any harm, might be a bit more ready to wash my hands if I was provided with a cloakroom like that in which to do so.

The lavatorium at Gloucester. *The wash place projects into the cloister garden, as it is too extensive and elaborate to house within the cloister walk.*

The lavatorium at Gloucester. *Would you believe that this was simply the place where the monks washed their hands before meals? Take away the trough and you could be in the cathedral itself.*

The Kitchen

onks' kitchens tend to be rather a disappointment; abbots' kitchens are often better. Once again, there is one outstanding example, this time at Glastonbury. There the kitchen now stands as an isolated building, shorn of all its connection with the former abbot's hall of which but a tiny fragment remains. The plan is basically square, with an octagonal roof surmounted by a lantern, and the chimneys in each corner would have led the smoke up and out.

Originally, when abbots slept in the dormitories, they would have eaten with the monks and been fed from the same kitchens, but their gradual separation from the general company led to the need for a separate kitchen, capable of serving visiting prelates or lay magnates and their retinues: hence Glastonbury. The monks' kitchen seems to have been about the same size, but no trace of it remains.

At Fountains (I'm sorry to be so constantly harking back there, but really it is the most extensive range of buildings and you can learn an enormous lot about monasteries from a visit to Fountains alone) there may have been four kitchens, although I don't know where the abbot's was. There are almost certainly three: a probable lay brothers' infirmary kitchen just to the south west of the hall; the main kitchen serving both monks and lay brothers through serving hatches in east and west walls respectively; and the infirmary kitchen which has a scullery attached, traces of ovens, and a delightful slop sink in one corner, directly over one of the principal drainage channels.

The principal kitchen was almost always in the south-west corner of the cloister, and in the case of Cistercian abbeys it usually was part of the south range, using the space gained by having the refectory running at right angles. These mostly followed the Fountains pattern of serving both lay and clerical monks, on opposite sides.

The abbot's kitchen at Glastonbury.
This is the outstanding surviving monastic kitchen, with its central vent for smoke and fumes.

Above: the abbot's kitchen at Glastonbury.
There are similar fireplaces, some with ovens set in the walls, in each corner of the building.

Left: the slop sink in the infirmary kitchen at Fountains.
Another fascinating domestic detail. This grill is directly over one of the drainage channels.

In monasteries without large establishments of lay brothers, the kitchen often filled the south-west angle itself, particularly in the early days, but later rebuildings often forced the expansion of the western range, so that the kitchen was displaced. This happened at both Thetford and Castle Acre priories, for example, where the kitchen moved further south, beyond the immediate claustral ring of buildings.

Although Glastonbury has its magnificent chimney corners – it is a fourteenth-century construction – the majority of monks' kitchens seem to have had a central hearth, with ovens at the sides of the room. Do not be deceived by the brick fireplace which one so frequently finds in various parts of monastic remains into thinking that a room with one in it is necessarily a kitchen (or a warming house); nor into assuming, even if it is the kitchen, that the chimney belongs to the monastic period. After the Romans left England, bricks really only came back into common building practice in the late fifteenth century, and very few monastic buildings were actually constructed of brick. (Even St Botolph's, Colchester, which might appear to be an exception, is mostly re-used Roman brick.) All those brick fireplaces are therefore usually signs of the post-Dissolution conversion into private dwelling houses which

The infirmary kitchen at Furness.
This must have been very similar to Glastonbury when complete.

Serving hatches at Monk
Bretton.
*These domestic details can bring
stern stones to life. Here is the
servery from the kitchen to the
refectory.*

overtook so many abbatial establishments, and the
brickwork cannot now be removed without bringing
most of its wall down with it.

There are often butteries and pantries associated
with the kitchens, just as in the great houses of the
period, and even that most vestigial of priories, Mattersey, has a serving hatch which appears to have
been from a buttery rather than the kitchen. By the
way, I only recently learnt that *buttery* and *butler*
both come from a French word connected with bottles.

The infirmary almost always had its own separate
kitchen. Apart from any other reason, meat could
only be eaten in the misericord (not to be confused
with the tip-up, prop-up, seats in the choir, although
the idea is the same: that of having pity on either the
long-standing monk or the infirm) and it was therefore
cooked in a separate place. I've already mentioned
the extensive example at Fountains, and the siting
and plan of the one at Furness are both interesting.

The simplicity of the monks' diet meant that the
kitchens did not need to be extensive or elaborate,
and the remains tend therefore to be scanty. Service
hatches, ovens, slop sinks and, as at Monk Bretton,
the clear pattern of the drainage can, however, add a
little more insight to your tour.

The Lay Brothers' or Cellarers' Range

The reason for the alternative title is not because there are two names for the same thing, as in so many cases such as frater/refectory, dorter/dormitory, farmery/infirmary, but because not every order of monks had lay brothers. If they did, then the whole western range was given over to them, but if they did not, then it was most often used for lay purposes, such as the storage of provisions.

It is ironical that for many people the most dramatic and evocative building of all monastic remains, churches excepted, is the undercroft of the lay brothers' range at Fountains. It is perhaps even more ironic that the stunning effect created today is because one sees that range as a whole, and not sub-divided as it originally was. When in use, there was a section used for storage; a central area walled off for the outer parlour, in which visitors were received and business transacted; and the lay brothers' refectory. Today one sees the entire 300-foot length in one great vista of vaults and columns.

It was a feature of some Cistercian monasteries that they provided for the lay brothers a down-market equivalent of the cloister, between the western alley of the monks' cloister and the west range itself. When you look at this walk at Byland today, with its dwarf walls and its neatly trimmed grass, it looks delightful, but it must have been distinctly less inviting when

Above: the lane at Byland.
This area was provided for the lay brothers to exercise in. When the walls on either side were at their full height it would not have looked so inviting.

Right: the lay brothers' undercroft at Fountains.
Formerly divided, this great space is now one of the most impressive monastic remains in the country.

those walls rose very much higher, with the church still higher at the northern end. Another good example of this kind of lane can be seen at Neath, while at Tintern an area much more similar to the usual cloister, although very much smaller, was provided west of the lay brothers' range and just to the north of the west front, since Tintern has its claustral buildings on the less common, northern side.

The lay brothers' dormitory ran along the west range at first floor level, just as that of the monks did in the east range. Even at Fountains, however, it is unlikely to have housed all the conversi (another name for the lay brothers) at any one time: many of them must have been away managing outlying farms, fisheries

The lay brothers' range at Fountains.
The lay brothers' dormitory stretched the whole first floor length of the building – and there would have been more elsewhere. The ground floor was more divided, as you can see from the various entrances, and a sort of porter's lodge was sited about half way along.

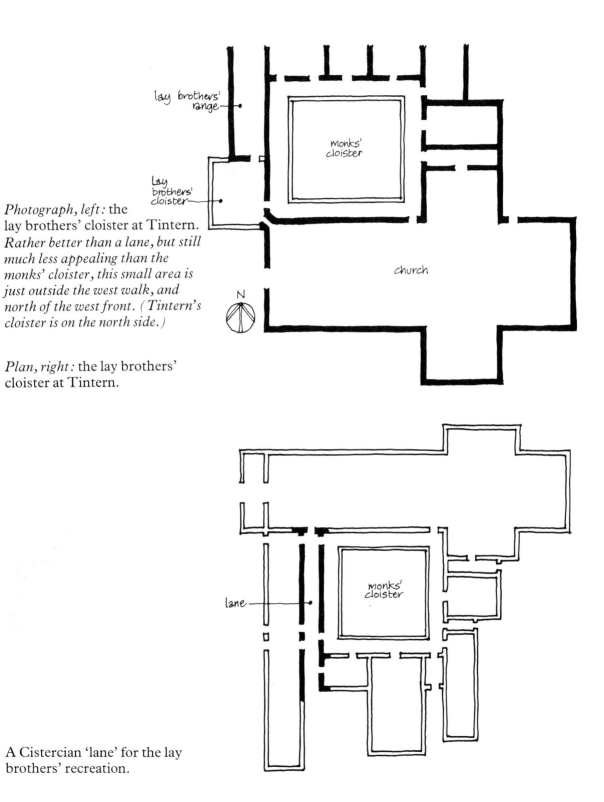

Photograph, left: the lay brothers' cloister at Tintern. *Rather better than a lane, but still much less appealing than the monks' cloister, this small area is just outside the west walk, and north of the west front. (Tintern's cloister is on the north side.)*

Plan, right: the lay brothers' cloister at Tintern.

A Cistercian 'lane' for the lay brothers' recreation.

and estates. When there is a lay brothers' dormitory and the church is long enough, one has the rare delight of a lay brothers' night stair. I hate to mention it yet again, but by far the best example I know is at Fountains. There the stair descends from the centre of the northern end of the dorter, and appears in the third bay of the south aisle. The flight appears complete, but is not accessible to the public. Often, the range is further west than the end of the church, and there the lay brothers would usually have a night stair close to the church, but not leading directly into it.

When there was no separate body of conversi to perform the more mundane tasks of the abbey, then the western range could be devoted entirely to storage and such purposes. In either case, the cellarer usually had a little office, either within or projecting outwards from the range, from which he could oversee all the multitudinous comings and goings which must have been necessary to supply the sometimes vast establishment for which he was responsible. There is a typical projecting porch at Castle Acre (no lay brothers) and an attached office at Tintern. At Monk Bretton, the outer parlour is linked to an inner gatehouse, which completely controlled access to the inner court of the priory.

Sometimes there was no substantial west range at all, merely a western wall enclosing the cloister. In those cases, and in some others as well, additional cellarage had to be found elsewhere about the monastery. The lie of the land at Rievaulx provided a useful undercroft to the frater, which was naturally at cloister level, while the rooms beneath could be used for storage. There are also some vats, used for dyeing, in a room at the same lower level, but I'm not sure whether they are monastic in date.

At Byland, the land falls much less steeply, although the cloister is well below the church. However, a split-level kind of arrangement was employed on the

The novices' room at Rievaulx. *No one is sure whether this was the novices' room, but it probably was. The brick structures are tanning vats.*

Above right: cellarage at Byland. The undercroft of the refectory is down a few steps from the cloister, so the refectory must have been up a few. The stonework in the foreground is racking for barrels.

south side of the cloister and, while the frater was five feet or so above cloister level, an undercroft which was partly below that level again provided ancillary accommodation: literally cellarage in this case, since you can see the racking for a row of barrels.

With the notable exception of Fountains, the cellarer's buildings do not tend to figure largely in the abbey ruin scene. They're not important like the church, the chapter house or the refectory. Nevertheless, where they survive, they often have rather interesting vaulting, while the odd little features I have already mentioned, such as the vats or the barrel racking, can all help to create a fuller picture of the flourishing monastery.

The Day Stair

Although I find the night stair more romantic, some monasteries didn't have one, and in any case all of them needed day stairs as well. With the huge dormitories of the Cistercians, these were very often situated in the south-east corner of the cloister, forming a kind of continuation of the east walk, but Cleeve has a winding stair in the middle of the east range, which therefore takes up space inside the dorter, whereas the other kind only needs a doorway.

Very often the stair runs parallel to the cloister, entered from a small porch to the south of the chapter house, but sometimes it is more like those found in some small modern terraced houses, where it leads off the hall/cloister walk at right angles and effectively separates the first floor into two halves. Unfortunately, the great dearth of upper storeys means that you very often only get the bottom step or two of a stairway and have to guess the rest, but I think that Kirkstall was of this type. Monk Bretton, too, probably had this sort of stair at first, but later rebuilding produced a very curious variant indeed. This was the insertion of a stair in the thickness of the wall of the south range, which therefore ran parallel to the south walk and at right angles to the dormitory, and presumably arrived at first floor level just as it reached the west wall of the latter.

I can't pretend that day stairs are a very important feature of monasteries, but they are yet another example of how fascinating variations on a theme can be. The day stair can be almost anywhere from close to the south transept to halfway along the south range, and it's fun looking for it.

The day stair at Cleeve.
A winding stair led up into the middle of the dormitory from the east cloister walk.

Right: the day stair at Fountains. *This stair, a continuation of the east cloister walk, reached the dormitory at almost the extreme eastern end, as far from the night stair as possible.*

Right: the day stair at Byland.
The stairway to the dormitory for use during the day leads off the east cloister walk at right angles and turns through another right angle to run up parallel to the walk until it reaches the upper floor.

The Dormitory

In the nature of things, there are fewer dormitories to look at than there are chapter houses, for example, and the remains are usually more fragmentary than those of, say, refectories. If a building is left to crumble, it usually crumbles from the top, and if it is being used as a quarry either by its new legitimate owner or by enterprising local lads, the stones at the top tend to be removed before those at the bottom. Even if the walls still stand, the roof has often gone.

At Battle Abbey you can, if you stand in the right place, and especially if you're taller than I am, see the whole length of the huge dorter, which was apparently still roofed in the eighteenth century. Today there is not even any access to this upper level for the interested visitor. Durham's dormitory is unusual in two respects: not only does it still retain its original roof timbers, but also it is over the western range of the cloister, whereas by far the most common position was the first floor of the eastern range, as an extension of the south transept. Not for the first time, however, in the examination of abbey remains, I find that the later use of the premises detracts from one's appreciation of the original fabric. The Durham dorter is now an impressive library and museum, and somehow therefore even the roofless Battle can be more evocative of the spartan monkish sleeping quarters.

Cleeve – again – provides an excellent example of a dormitory, but even there restoration has been undertaken which, I am inclined to think, may have taken away a little of the magic. Of course, I may only think that because it has changed from the state in which I first saw it: perhaps if I came new to it, or if I had seen it some time before what happened to be my first visit, I would take a different attitude. Anyway, when I did go for the first time, only half the dormitory floor was there, and now it all is. At least this enables you to inspect the south-east angle, where the passage

The east range at Battle.
The monks' dormitory lay behind the two tall narrow windows, with the reredorter or lavatory block running off to the right. The sloping site means that the other end is much easier to see into.

to the reredorter used to be, and you can see the niche where the lantern used to hang at night to guide the monks if they had to relieve themselves during the hours of darkness.

Originally, the abbot was supposed to sleep in the dormitory with his monks, and to be truly *primus inter pares*, but gradually he became more detached from the common herd and withdrew, first of all to his own room or cell, and eventually to his own house or lodging. Sometimes you can find evidence of tenuous links intended to pay lip service to the earlier ideal,

The dormitory at Cleeve.
In the middle is the day stair, and at the far end on the left was the reredorter.

and the abbot's lodging will be connected to the dorter by a passage, or will share the use of the reredorter.

As the abbot grew away from the monks, so the latter grew away from each other, and the dormitories came to be divided into little cubicles by wooden partitions. These have long since vanished and, although I believe that traces can sometimes be seen of their existence, I can't think of a single example to point out to you.

An interesting feature – features – of the dormitory which can usually be traced is the access. In many monasteries there are two stairways, the day stair and the night stair. The night stair I have told you quite a lot about in the chapter on the church, from which it rises, but on the comparatively rare occasions when you can visit a dorter it is fun to look for the night stair going the other way, down into the church. Of course, in many cases that is how you will have reached the dorter in the first place, as at Dryburgh, but on the other hand at Cleeve, where the church has entirely disappeared, you can see the doorway inside the dormitory, but beyond it – nothing. There, you gain access by a twisting little day stair that comes up out of the eastern cloister walk.

In many of the large Cistercian monasteries in particular, the dorter is reached by a day stair continuing beyond the end of the eastern walk, and it rises parallel to that range, between it and the southern buildings such as the warming house. That is the arrangement at Fountains, and also at Neath, but in the latter case the complete disappearance of the warming house (and the conversion of the dormitory range into a post-Reformation house) means that the stair is hardly recognisable.

There must be an example somewhere of a dorter which you can enter by the day stair and leave by the night stair (or vice versa). Unfortunately, I can't think of it.

The Reredorter

he reredorter is simply the monks' lavatory or latrine. I've already told you not to get confused with the lavatorium, which is where the monks washed their hands before eating, and I repeat that warning here. It all comes from the English reluctance to call a spade a spade, and the desire to find a euphemism for the place where one excretes. Anyway, that necessary place in the monastery was called the reredorter, and was attached by some means or other to the dorter.

The most usual position was at right angles to the end furthest from the church, but there are variants. At Neath the reredorter is parallel to the dormitory, almost certainly because of the drainage runs, and is linked to it by a bridge about half way along. At Battle it is in the usual position, and is a very long narrow projection. Sometimes, as at Castle Acre, it runs across the foot of the dormitory, which may have saved diverting the drain too much to the north.

Something that has always puzzled me is that the latrines seem only to have existed at first floor level. There are occasional odd garderobes on the ground floor – Hailes, and later alterations at Cleeve – but there does not seem to have been a ground-floor range, accessible from the day room, similar to that reached from the dormitory. I don't known whether this means that the monks' lives were so well-ordered that they only needed the lavatories when they were in the dormitory, or whether they simply had to go via the dorter when they needed them, or whether they made other arrangements. Perhaps they, too, employed a euphemism: 'I've just got to go upstairs'.

I also don't know how the range of closets, being on the upper storey, were 'flushed' or kept clean. The disposal at ground level is obvious, and well ordered. The latrines fed into a channel which was flushed by part of the complicated system of streams and drains which every monastery had, and was then led back

The dormitory at Cleeve. *Where the reredorter (now vanished) joined the dormitory through the arch on the left, there was a niche to hold a lantern, to light the monks' way from the dormitory.*

The reredorter at Muchelney. *Now a farm shed. The drainage channels for the monk's lavatory block can be seen below the building.*

into the main river below the kitchen and fresh water outlets.

Although the reredorter block consisted of a row of lavatory seats, they may have been divided by wooden partitions, and the monk was supposed to cover his face with his cowl when going to or using them. It wasn't meant to be a communal activity, and I can't resist quoting an odd case which I found in a book of fourteenth-century law suits. A man in the City of London was required to repair the wall between his privy and next door because 'the extremities of those sitting upon the seats can be seen, a thing which is abominable'. I don't suppose that the inhabitants of monasteries were any more in favour of viewing their neighbours' extremities.

Nowadays, what can mostly be seen is the drain, and sometimes the sub-structure of the block. Very occasionally a substantial building will remain, as at Muchelney, but I don't know of any remains which are so clearly indicative of their purpose as, for example, the Roman latrine at Housesteads.

Various Other Rooms

 ther chapters have dealt with rooms or buildings which you can expect to find in every – or nearly every – monastery. There are some different rooms, however, which crop up here and there, making a particular site more interesting than it otherwise might be. Some of them – the novices' room, the sacristy, and the parlour, for example – will probably be within the claustral group, and others may be scattered about the monastic court.

Prisons, for example. These were sometimes part of the abbey's lay jurisdiction, and might therefore be found in gatehouses, but the cells at Fountains appear to have been for recalcitrant monks. Other examples are:

Novices' room When in doubt about a ground floor room, south of the chapter house in the east range, call it a novices' room. After all, they had to learn somewhere.

Almonry Sometimes an outbuilding but often part of a gatehouse, used for dispensing alms to the poor.

Garderobes Individual lavatories, found in abbots' lodgings, some late cells (monastic, not prison – at least I think so) underneath the frater at Cleeve, and at odd places elsewhere: more common in castles.

Treasury Many monasteries needed a small separate room in which to secure their valuables, and it seems often to have been close to the dormitory or the sacristy. I can't say that I can ever remember seeing it, but I've read that the Fountains' treasury clearly exists between the chapter house and south transept, at first floor level. You can't visit it at present, however.

Sacristy I've mentioned sacristies elsewhere without making clear what they are: administrative offices from which the sacristan ran the maintenance of the church building and its fittings, which usually adjoined the south transept, or the south side of the presbytery.

Parlour There were often two parlours, places where speech was permitted: an outer, usually in the west

The night stair and treasury at Kirkstall.
The little low door on the left, on the landing just outside the doorway into the transept, serves a very small room. It is almost certainly the treasury of the abbey.

A scriptorium(?) at Wenlock.
In the south west corner of the nave is an upper room – the two large windows shown here. It may have been set aside for the monks to write in.

range, where necessary negotiations with the outside world could take place; and an inner, where the monks could speak to each other about the business of the abbey. The latter was not often very big, and was usually in the east range, near the chapter house.

Scriptorium In the chapter on the cloister I have explained that most English monasteries had no special room set aside for writing and copying books but probably used the arms of the cloister for such work, frequently dividing the walk into small cubicles known as carrels. However, some evidence does seem to exist that there were a few rooms for that particular purpose, and it has been argued that the unidentified room over the south aisle at Wenlock might be a scriptorium. (Others say that it is a chapel to St Michael.) St Albans claims to have had one, but I don't know of any evidence for it.

There are a few other rooms which you may come across, but the above list should at least give you some idea what to look out for.

The Infirmary

ick monks were cared for within the curtilage of their own monastery, and the infirmarer was one of the senior officers of the organisation. As many monks came to the cloister after an active life outside, as well as those who had joined as young novices, there tended to be a disproportionate number of the elderly, although no doubt the lack of modern scientific aids meant that they did not linger as long in this world as the elderly of today. In addition, many abbeys cared for the sick in general, and those rich laymen who had bought corrodies (a sort of annuity) would probably expect to end their days in the farmery.

In the larger monasteries, therefore, the infirmary was a fairly big building, and in those establishments that had a large number of conversi, there would be a lay brothers' infirmary as well. Not surprisingly, Fountains has a good example of each type. The main infirmary was to the east of the cloister, its most usual position, and was an enormous hall, with its own kitchen, chapel, and meat dining hall or misericord (not to be confused with the tip-up choir seat of the same name): for health reasons, the sick were allowed to eat meat more often than the rest of the monks, and this was done in a special room set aside for the purpose.

The hall at Fountains is about 180 by 78 feet, and must have been one of the largest buildings of its type and time. Probably the Hall of the Knights in Rhodes gives a good impression of what it may have been like originally or, on a much smaller scale, the Bedesmen's Hall at Higham Ferrers. Just as the monks originally slept in a common dormitory, so did the infirm, and probably the partitioning off of individual spaces took place at much the same time, providing private wards in the great hall. With its ancillary buildings, the infirmary at Fountains is probably as big as many a monastery.

Bottom: the infirmary at Thetford.
The pebbled area in the right foreground is the central garth; two of the walks can be seen, with infirmary rooms around them.

The infirmary at Furness.
The new infirmary was very large to the south of the cloister. The two-storey building at the east end contains a chapel and the serving area adjoining the kitchen.

Quite a contrast is the infirmary at Thetford, which is built just like a small cloister, but really is tiny: the whole thing could fit into the cloister garth of the priory. There is a central paved courtyard, with four buildings ranged around it, of which the hall and the chapel have been identified.

At Furness, the early infirmary was in the usual position, but this later became the abbot's lodging, while the farmery moved to a new position, south of the cloister and roughly parallel to the church. The new hall was much larger, and had a chapel and kitchen (a most attractive octagon) abutting its eastern end.

As you can see, the infirmary tended to be less rigid in its positioning than most of the other monastic buildings, and in Netley it even seems to have been part of the undercroft to the dorter and reredorter. However, it is usually to be found to the east of the east range, and south of the presbytery, but looking for it is part of the fun of exploring the site of any abbey for the first time.

The Abbot's Lodging

If you read the history of the monastic orders you will find that each new order tended to be a revolt against the laxity into which the previous orders had fallen. Good intentions often fell away, frequently for the most justifiable of reasons. Whereas it was quite reasonable to suggest in primitive societies that the abbot should live with his fellow monks, being superior to them only in that he had been chosen to be their spiritual leader, both spiritual pride and temporal demands soon began to lead him into a very different way of life. Quite apart from the natural tendency of any leader to begin to think that he is different from those he is leading, which all we natural leaders have to fight against, the important

part which the abbots of the larger monasteries began to play in national life meant that they had to have somewhere separate in which to live and to entertain important guests.

In some abbeys, they maintained a tenuous link to the common dormitory, but in many they hived themselves off to a completely separate building. At Castle Acre, the prior had a charming suite of rooms in the west range, which projects forward of the arcaded west front of the church. There was a solar, a chapel, and a hall, with some rooms probably used in common with the adjoining guest hall. As was often the case, these apartments were a natural choice for conversion to residential occupation after the Dissolution, and so

Above: Castle Acre, prior's solar. *The bow window can be seen on the exterior photograph. This room formed part of a small suite, and served as a sort of living room.*

Below: Castle Acre, west front. *This photograph shows not only the Norman arcading of the west front, but also the prior's lodging with its bow window, projecting forward of the church.*

The abbot's lodging at Kirkstall. *The great stair serving the first floor hall of the three-storey building. You can only get this view by special permission or by being slim enough to slip through the railings.*

are now in better repair than the rest of the priory. They have also, of course, undergone considerable alterations. At Muchelney, the lodging was in the south range, and actually sat over the cloister walk in a most unusual way.

Kirkstall and Fountains both had abbots' lodgings joined to the monks' dorter by the reredorter (the tenuous link of which I spoke above), and the former, dating from *c.*1230, appears to be a very fine example – if one could only get close enough to examine it. Very often, the gradual socially-upward movement of the abbot meant that he occupied different buildings successively: indeed many buildings changed their position or function during their hundreds of years of existence. Thus, at Furness, the abbot took over the

The abbot's lodging/infirmary at Furness.
Changes in ways of living meant that buildings frequently changed their use. When a new infirmary was erected, this building became the abbot's lodging.

former infirmary building when its occupants moved to their later site.

The abbot's house at Tewkesbury projects westward from the church, almost forming a continuation of the south aisle. This building is occupied to this day, but the south front was so remodelled in the eighteenth century that you would never recognise its monastic origins from this aspect.

Those abbeys whose churches became cathedrals very naturally turned lodgings into accommodation for the bishops, deans and other clerics who took over the running of the establishment. Peterborough and Winchester are but two cathedrals where several of the early buildings have been adapted in this way. Elsewhere, the abbots' halls, which were usually first-floor buildings, have tended to go the way of many first-floor buildings: first to be robbed, and first to crumble. Remember, when looking for or finding them, that they may at some time have received the great lords of the land, perhaps even the king himself, if they were the only suitable housing to be found in the area which the king wanted to visit. When you think that all his retinue would have to be fed and looked after as well, you can understand why some abbeys have very extensive accommodation both for the abbot and for his guests.

Outbuildings

Abbeys very soon became rich landowners. Local magnates, hoping to put themselves on the right side of God, or at least His earthly representatives, would make donations of land, or might purchase corrodies (sheltered housing in their old age) by handing over part of their estates. Sometimes these lands might be close around the monastery, but often they would be a day or more's journey distant. It is very hard for us today to appreciate just what distance meant in the Middle Ages. Perhaps the best analogy I can think of from my own experience comes from taking a canal holiday. Two days after we had set out, something fell off the engine, and we had to telephone to the yard for assistance. In less than an hour an engineer had arrived by road to repair it. It must have been rather like that in pre-Industrial Revolution Britain: two days' travel to reach somewhere which we think of as just up the road.

The result of this was that whenever lands had to be managed which were more than a few miles from the monastery, some accommodation had to be provided for the monks to stay overnight. With the more distant estates, the monks might live there for some considerable time. If you read the detective stories of Ellis Peters, featuring a monk of Shrewsbury named Cadfael, you will come across some of these outposts.

The most dramatic buildings which resulted from the collection of supplies in distant parts are the tithe barns. Strictly speaking, I suppose, only a barn used to hold produce given in tithe by parishioners should be so described, but it has become a generic term for large mediaeval barns. Certainly the great barn at Bradford-on-Avon, which held the output of local farming, was part of a grange belonging to an abbey some distance away in Shaftesbury, and grange barn is a more correct term. The barn at Titchfield, on the other hand, is just outside the abbey gates – and now houses a farm shop.

Right: the interior of the grange barn at Bradford-on-Avon.
The farm implements stored inside give some idea of the massive size of such structures.

Below right: the barn at Tisbury. *Now part of a private farm, this is said to be the largest barn in England. Mediaeval abbeys were great farmers, and needed large stores for their produce.*

Below: the grange barn at Bradford-on-Avon.
The exterior view does not convey the great size, only the grandeur of this building.

The warren house at Thetford.
In order to look after his outlying lands and possessions, the abbot had small lodgings such as this one, where a couple of monks could live to tend the rabbits.

Fish formed a large part of the monks' diet, and the fisheries too needed convenient buildings. The abbot's fish house can be seen at Meare, not far from the official seat of the abbot at Glastonbury – and I think he had a residence for himself at Meare as well. Very often, by the way, there were fish ponds within the abbey precinct and therefore needing no special outbuildings. Strictly speaking, those are outside the ambit of this chapter, but I don't see where else they're going to get mentioned, so you may care to look out for them.

Another source of food was rabbits, and some previously obscure buildings have now been recognised as the warren lodges of lords and abbeys. Apparently

Above: the barn at Leonard Stanley.
The gable over the doorway contains a rare surviving dovecot.

Left: the abbot's fish house at Meare (Glastonbury).
As the house at Thetford was provided for farming rabbits, so this one was for tending the fisheries.

the rabbits were positively farmed, and these buildings, one of which can be seen at Thetford, were constructed to serve as the farmhouses for that purpose. Doves were also bred, and there is a monastic dovecot at Penmon in Anglesey.

I don't know whether hermitages properly come within the scope of this book, let alone this chapter, but this is as good a place to mention them as any. After all, they are a sort of embryo monastery and, as the history chapter explains, some early monasteries were collections of hermitages. The best example I know is at Warkworth, near the castle, and you get a ferry across the river to see quite an impressive set of rooms cut into the rocky bank.

A comparative rarity is the court room, used by the great abbots in their capacity as feudal lords. The Tribunal at Glastonbury is perhaps the best example.

The Tribunal at Glastonbury. *In this building, a short distance from the monastery, the abbot exercised his lay judiciary powers.*

So far in this chapter, I have only dealt with distant outbuildings, but there were likely to be many in the immediate vicinity of the monastery itself, even though comparatively few of them have survived. They were all too easily laicised at the Dissolution, and then subsequently knocked down or rebuilt, in the normal way of domestic buildings.

Since every abbey had its own stream, what more natural than that it should have its own mill? I believe there is a monastic mill at Abingdon, but I have only seen the one at Fountains, which is missed by most people, since it is out of sight behind some trees as you come through the entrance gate, and as your attention is then caught by the west end of the abbey, you walk straight ahead instead of striking off sharply to the right. Even I didn't see it till my sixth visit or thereabouts.

Even if they hadn't had their own mills, the abbeys

The mill at Fountains.
In a bad way structurally, to judge from the shoring, the mill stands only a short distance from the main abbey buildings, using the same stream which provided all the abbey's water.

would have had their own bakehouses. Sometimes these are closely associated with the kitchens, but in other cases they are more distant. Since bread formed a substantial part of the monks' diet, the bakehouse must have been a very busy place. Few remains are visible, and even at Fountains where there are some, it is hard to disentangle them from the undergrowth.

The other staple of the monks, much though it revolts me as a teetotaller to have to mention it, was beer, and at Fountains the malthouse adjoins the bakehouse. There is an excellent brewery at Lacock, but it is post-Dissolution: even so, it probably gives you a good idea of what a monastic brewhouse might have been like.

Outbuildings come in many shapes and forms, and some of them may be of such forms and so separated from their monastic parents that they are hard to recognise as having any abbatial connections. The few that do exist, however, help to give an insight into mediaeval life as a whole, and not just that of the abbey of which they form a separated part.

Gatehouses

s may be becoming obvious to you as you read this book, so many buildings went to make up a great monastery that it was almost like a small town. As such, it was surrounded by a precinct wall, and entry was only through the gatehouse. Many of these gatehouses have survived in very good condition because they were so readily adaptable to other uses after the Dissolution. Some of them are still serving secular purposes; some are monuments to their former use; and some are fragmentary ruins.

Kirkstall gatehouse, which is now separated from its abbey by a busy main road, first of all sheltered its deposed abbot and now houses a folk museum with streets of old shops, and a collection of penny-in-the-slot toys, including a polyphon. Wonder of wonders, you can even obtain a supply of old-fashioned pennies to make them work.

Thornton has a magnificent fourteenth-century example, to judge from its photograph in the *English Heritage Guide*, and I can praise from my own knowledge the buildings at St Albans and Battle. St Osyth, whose flinty appearance partly reminds me of St Albans, has become part of a stately home, but the other abbey remains there are very slight.

Below: the gatehouse of St Albans.
Not quite so ruined by Victorianisation as the rest of the cathedral, the gatehouse still presents a formidable appearance.

Right: the gatehouse at Canterbury.
More ornate than St Albans, this proclaimed the status of the abbey to the townsfolk. The side door could be opened for pedestrians when the vehicular door was shut.

Worksop gatehouse has been used, at least until recently, as offices for a local engineering firm and Bridlington offers a small local museum. Those are two cases where the only thing that is left of the abbey, apart from the church (or part of it) is the gatehouse. Cartmel is another, but Kingswood goes one further: there only the gatehouse survives, with not even a church to keep it company.

Although the ruins of Fountains are so extensive, the fact that they have been incorporated into a deliberate landscaping tends to obscure the size of the abbey precinct. This can be best appreciated, I think, at Bury St Edmunds where the finest two standing buildings are St James' Gate and The Great Gate. One guarded the entrance to the abbey church, and the other served the great outer court. From the latter, a further gate was controlled by the cellarer and led back towards the church. At least two other gateways existed, including one for the abbot convenient to his palace. It is ironical that so many gates should have featured in the precinct wall of Bury, since relations between the monastery and the town appear to have been about the worst anywhere. The monks may have needed gates, but those gates needed to be very defensible.

Paradoxically, where substantial ruins of the claustral buildings survive, the gatehouse is often less well preserved. At Cleeve and Roche, for example, although its function is perfectly obvious, the building itself is not very inspiring. However, there is always a special pleasure in making one's approach to the ruins through such a gateway, however exiguous. You can really feel that you are following the steps of the thousands who must have come that way in the abbey's heyday.

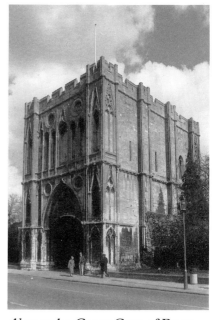

Above: the Great Gate of Bury St Edmunds.
This one dates from the fourteenth century.

Right: St James' Gate at Bury St Edmunds.
There were several gateways into the monastery, and this one is early twelfth century. Ironically, the gates are the best preserved parts of the abbey.

Guest Houses

s I have explained while dealing with the abbot's lodging, it was often necessary for an abbey to act as host to a large party of visiting dignitaries and their entourage: Henry VI stayed for eight weeks at Bury St Edmunds in 1433. This, however, was the exception, but it was at all times the duty of an abbey to house the ordinary visitor, especially a pilgrim, for a night or two. All monasteries therefore made provision for such tasks, although it might vary from a couple of rooms in the western range, to a massive building well away from the abbey proper so that the more noisy guests did not disturb the quiet of the cloister.

At Castle Acre, where some of the accommodation was used in common with the abbot, the guests were housed in two small chambers above the west range. At Kirkstall, on the other hand, there is a vast building – although only foundations remain – containing a hall, chamber, kitchen and stables, about the size of the nave of the church and situated a short distance from the west front.

The guest house at St Mary's, York (from which certain disaffected brethren went off to found Fountains) is a rectangular block now housing part of the Yorkshire Museum, although it isn't open to the public at present. One of my reference books says that guests were housed in the west range and entertained in the south range, but although the ruins are extremely scanty, the building which I have been led to believe is the guest house hardly fits with either of those – although it must be nearer to the west range than anything else.

The same book says that there is a complete guest house of the Knights Hospitaller at Anstey (*sic*) in Wiltshire. Astonishing as this may seem, I have never been there, but if I visit it before publication I will try to include a photograph.

In many ways, the guest houses which are most

The guest house at Malmesbury. *Almost a continuation of the nave, the building where distinguished visitors were housed is now a hotel which even you or I can visit.*

The George Inn at Norton St Philip.
This was either the guest house of Hinton Charterhouse, or possibly housed monks during the building. Either way, it is a most interesting building to examine.

fun to visit are those which still fulfil the same function – more or less. Two, at least, spring readily to mind. The first is The Old Bell Hotel in Malmesbury. This stands in the same relationship to the church as does the abbot's house at Tewkesbury: a sort of prolongation of the nave beyond the west front. The remains are not easy to see, and the hotel is very much a hotel (much the nicest in the town), but it's very pleasant if visiting the abbey to stay on the site where former visitors spent the night.

The best example, if true, is at Hinton Charterhouse. Unfortunately, some doubt surrounds the origins of the building, but The George at Norton St Philip is said to have been a guest house of the charterhouse about one mile away. It is entirely believable that an enclosed order would have supported a guest house at some distance from the priory, although the one at Mount Grace is adjacent to the cloister. I like to believe it, because it is a lovely old building, of about the right period, with a galleried courtyard (only accessible during opening hours) and a nice line in vegetarian lunches.

Just in case you thought you were going to have a chapter with no more than an oblique reference to Fountains, I should mention that there the guest house is close to the lay brothers' infirmary, and consists of two substantial wings with a yard between.

Charterhouses

 espite having told you that I wasn't going to mention what one might call sectarian differences, I think that Carthusians are so special that I'm going to have to give them their own chapter. They led an altogether different lifestyle from the rest of the monkish fraternity: even the differences between the preaching orders and the contemplative ones (i.e., the Franciscans and Augustinians on the one hand, and the Benedictines, Cistercians and Cluniacs on the other) are as nothing compared with the differences between the lot of them and the Carthusians. The church was not the central focus of activity in the same way at all, and instead of spending most of their time in communal worship, the monks spent it in solitary contemplation in their individual cells.

The word 'cell' conjures up a prison-like image in most people's minds and, indeed, many cells in more 'open' – to continue the prison metaphor – monasteries are rather like that. But a Carthusian cell is a jolly sight bigger than the houses in which many people live today.

There is only one place in England nowadays where you can get any idea of what a charterhouse looked like, and that is Mount Grace in Yorkshire. A complete cell has been restored (I think it was originally done to act as a garden shed: certainly for many years when I visited it, it seemed to be full of mowers and ladders and suchlike) and you could see that it offered four very reasonably sized rooms, but unfortunately, no sooner had they opened the restored cell than they shut it again. On my last visit, the whole thing was shrouded in scaffolding. Admittedly the lavatory is at the bottom of the garden – oh yes, there's a garden too – and there's no bathroom or kitchen, but then food was brought to each monk's cell and given to him through a serving hatch.

This serving hatch is one of the delights in all

A cell at Mount Grace.
This desirable detached residence formed the living quarters of a single Carthusian monk.

A garderobe at Mount Grace.
Individual lavatories were provided at the end of the garden attached to each cell in a charterhouse. You obviously had to duck to get into the lavatory, which was flushed by the general water supply. The drain from the cell can be seen on the right.

charterhouses. (I know I've just said that there's only one good place in England, but there are lots more abroad. In France they are called *chartreuses*, and there's an excellent example at Villeneuve-lès-Avignon, just across the river from the famous *Pont*, and getting about one-hundredth of the visitors who crowd the famous Palace of the Popes. I believe that the mother house, the *Grande Chartreuse*, still functions, but I've never been there. In Italy you have to look for a *certosa*, and there's a good one in Naples, and another just outside Florence. I believe there's an excellent one near Milan, but I haven't been there yet. In Spain it's a *cartuja*, and there's one at Granada, if you can tear yourself away from that city's other delights. Sorry about the long parenthesis: back to England.) In order that the Carthusian monk could continue his meditation completely undisturbed by human contact, his meals were brought by a lay brother and passed through a right-angled opening, so that neither could see the other.

Not very many complete right-angles remain, but they're very interesting when found.

Because of the size of each cell, and the fact that its garden also partly abutted the cloister, there isn't room for many monks even round an enormous cloister, far bigger than that of any other order, and so sometimes secondary cloisters spring up, as at Mount Grace, usually with the cells a bit tighter packed, but even so the number of Carthusians was never great.

Since the church was not the focus of the Carthusian's daily round, it is not the grand building to be found elsewhere – and, of course, it didn't have to accommodate so many people. There was no question of parishioners here, and the community itself was small.

Apart from Mount Grace, the traces to be found in England are small indeed, and have recently become even less accessible. Hinton Charterhouse (the name of the village) has a complete chapter house and sacristy which used to be open to visitors occasionally. At the time of writing it is completely closed, but you can see the exterior from the A36. Very much open to the public is Hinton's possible outbuilding, The George at Norton St Philip, which is described a little more fully in the chapter on guest houses.

Apart from the church of Witham, not far away from Hinton, which is rather boring and only recommendable to addicts, that only leaves the eponymous London Charterhouse, which is a fine collection of old buildings in which it is very difficult indeed to detect the pattern of the conventual buildings. Have a try, though, if you get the opportunity.

To sum up, then: if you want to get any impression in England of a charterhouse, you'll have to make the trek to Osmotherley unless you're lucky enough to live close by already, but it's well worth it. Meanwhile, keep your eyes open abroad, where charterhouses are rather more thick on the ground.

A Carthusian cell, with the feeding arrangement.

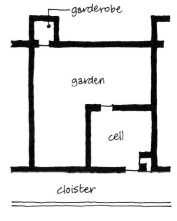

PLAN

monk takes food from inside cell

cell door

lay brother delivers food from cloister

DETAIL PLAN OF DELIVERY HATCH

The chapter house of Hinton Charterhouse.
The only substantial remains of this priory, no longer on view to the public except from the A36.

A Short History of the English Monastery

hen we hear the word monastery, we reach into our minds for an image of a typical Benedictine or Cistercian group of buildings, such as I have described in the chapter on *The Abbey as a Whole*. Indeed, this image and the basic story of the mediaeval abbey are so clear in my mind that I wasn't going to put any history into this book at all, until I realised that the odd references to events such as the Dissolution of the Monasteries really needed to be set in context.

You will find a reference to St Augustine's Abbey at Canterbury in the *Gazetteer*, if nowhere else, which can be described as the first 'Roman' monastery in England. The distinction is necessary, because there was a considerable Celtic Christian presence in England before St Augustine arrived in 597. Many schoolboys are familiar with (one used to be able to say with confidence: 'Every schoolboy knows . . .') the story of Pope Gregory the Great who, seeing some fair-haired captives in Rome enquired who they were and, being told that they were Angli (Anglo-Saxons) made his famous pun, saying 'Non Angli sed Angeli'. (Not Anglo-Saxons but Angels.) He then sent St Augustine to convert the heathen English. (This Augustine, the better known to British audiences, must not be confused with the greater figure on the world stage, St Augustine of Hippo, whose rule the Augustinian Canons were later to follow. The African bishop's most quoted utterance is his reputed early prayer, 'Lord, give me chastity and continence, but not yet'.)

It was one thing to convert the heathen: it was quite another to win over the already converted Christians from their Celtic allegiance. Although the differences were only of doctrine and practice, not of basic

The Saxon church at Bradford-on-Avon.
It seems that this tiny church may have had pre-Norman monastic connections. It's worth a visit anyway.

faith, sectarianism to this day – in Ulster, to quote but the most prominent example – demonstrates how hard these small bridges are to cross. Eventually, the Synod of Whitby in 664 came down on the side of Rome, and is almost the only justification for the lengthy journey (from most parts of England) to see the very fragmentary remains of the later abbey, dramatic though they may look on their cliff top.

Celtic monasticism, brought to Britain from Ireland via Iona, had been quite widespread before the 'Roman Invasion' including, ironically, a probable site at Whitby. Their monasteries were basically composed of a collection of hermitages, with the occasional communal room. Only scanty remains of any of these establishments still exist: at Tintagel can be seen scattered foundations on a site even more dramatic than Whitby.

What we, and certainly I, really tend to think of as monasteries followed on from the Norman Conquest. Although there were forty or so Benedictine monasteries in England in 1066, they were all to undergo profound changes and substantial rebuilding in the ensuing years. Jarrow – home of the Venerable Bede, from whose most famous work the title of this chapter is adapted – was an Anglo-Saxon Benedictine foundation, some of whose remains can still be distinguished because it did not become a great mediaeval abbey, but most of the early buildings have completely disappeared.

It was the flood of ecclesiastics who followed in the train of William the Conqueror who rebuilt nearly all the early monasteries and founded many new ones, most – if not all – Benedictine. The name, by the way, in each case indicates the person or monastery according to whose rule the particular establishment had decided to live, and St Benedict provided the first such rule to win wide allegiance.

I will not weary you with a complex description of the politics of the various orders, but the main line consisted of a succession of reforms to the basic Benedictine rule: first Cluniac (from Cluny) and then Cistercian (from Cîteaux). Various parallel lines were followed by such as the Gilbertines, while Premonstratersians seem to have been a halfway house between Cistercians and Friars. The Friars, among them prominently Dominicans, Augustinians and Carmelites, were much more outgoing and evangelical. Their huge preaching churches can be seen to best advantage in such places as Venice (SS Giovanni e Paolo and The Frari) and Florence (S Croce and S Maria Novella). The Knights, Hospitaller and Templar, arose from the Crusades and provided help and protection to pilgrims. Carthusians have already had a chapter to themselves.

At their peak, the great monasteries were virtually small townships, the extent of which can be well appreciated at Bury St Edmunds. In the middle of the twelfth century, there were 140 monks and over 500 lay brothers at Rievaulx, while the numbers at Fountains and Kirkstall at least must have been similar. I don't know the population of the largest nunnery, but Romsey must be in the running for that title and it housed 90 nuns in 1333, which was probably after

The west front of Margam. *A typically simple Cistercian west end.*

it had passed its greatest size. All the abbeys and priories suffered considerable losses in numbers from outside influences such as the Black Death and the Hundred Years' War, as well as from declining enthusiasm for the monastic life, so that by the sixteenth century, very few of them were anything like their original size. It is to the decline in numbers at Cleeve that we owe the building of the fine new first-floor refectory in the late fifteenth century, which meant that the tiled floor for the late thirteenth-century frater was covered with earth to be rediscovered for our modern delight. At Rievaulx, to point the contrast, there were but 22 monks at the Dissolution.

The decline in numbers was one factor seized upon by Henry VIII to justify closing down ecclesiastical institutions, although in fact the reasons were much more complicated, springing partly from his declaration of the independence of the Church of England and of himself as Supreme Head of that Church. Even this was not so much a doctrinal as a political and dynastic matter. Whatever the reason, the effect was that the King's commissioners went round examining the finances of all the monasteries. In 1536 all religious houses with an income of less than £200 per annum were closed, and in subsequent years all the others followed, no matter what their financial position was, the last to fall being Waltham in 1540.

Those abbots and monks who resisted the King were hanged, but many of those who went quietly were given generous pensions. Some of them removed to ecclesiastical posts elsewhere – often abroad – and the abbot of Kirkstall is said to have retired to his own gatehouse for the rest of his life.

After the Dissolution, most of the monastic buildings were sold off by the King (the money thus raised being another compelling reason for the exercise) to local – or more distant – land owners and magnates.

Lacock Abbey.
Contrast this view of the 'Gothick'
entrance with the view of the
cloister behind. This was the view
intended for the arriving visitor at
the stately home.

In some cases, parishes which had been accustomed to worship there bought all or part of the monastic church. The lay purchaser either used the building as a convenient quarry for cut and dressed stone, to employ in building for himself or to sell off, or converted the buildings themselves into a residence. Netley and Titchfield are two good examples of house conversions which are now ruined and look more like abbeys again, while Forde and Lacock are still standing domestic buildings, of which the latter is a remarkable example of a structure which looks all stately home on the outside, but contains substantial remains of the nunnery concealed within. If the purchaser neglected the buildings altogether, time and opportunistic locals soon began their depredations.

These three fates for the abbey, destruction, conversion and neglect, have reduced nearly all the fantastic range of establishments which existed at the beginning of the sixteenth century to little more than foundations and fragments. Disentangling the fragments from later accretions and rebuilding upon the foundations, in the mind at least, are among the great joys of abbey exploring.

Present-Day Monasteries

As I have walked round the sites of mediaeval monasteries I have often wondered, and perhaps you may too, how closely their modern counterparts resemble them. I have always felt diffident about going up to the door of an abbey, with no religious justification, and simply asking for information. Recently, however, I had the opportunity of talking to a former monk from an English monastery, and so in case some of my readers share my curiosity I will set out a little of what I learned from him.

I was surprised to discover how many Benedictine monasteries there are in England today: sixteen Roman Catholic establishments of monks and seventeen of nuns; and two Anglican houses of monks and six of nuns. It seems that Benedictines are still, as they were in the Middle Ages, slightly more relaxed in their discipline than some other orders. They rise at 5 a.m., while the Cistercians begin their day at 3.30 a.m. Is this why there is only one Cistercian house in each of England, Wales and Scotland? There is only one Carthusian priory in the whole of the United Kingdom.

Silence is still observed at meal times, and in general in Cistercian abbeys, but the readings from the refectory pulpit in Benedictine houses may well include modern secular works as well as passages from scripture. Sign language for use in asking your neighbour to pass various items of food is much as it was, but new signs have had to be invented for such luxury items as marmalade.

When monasteries thrived in the Middle Ages they were seats of learning, and many still were so even when calumnies were flying about concerning their back-sliding and their luxurious living (not to mention the hoary old joke: what fun does a monk have? Nun!). When Roman Catholics were relieved of civil disabilities in England in 1829 they were still not allowed to go to university and they were not over-keen on exposing their postulants to the likely temptations there, either. The nineteenth and early twentieth-century monks were often, therefore, not very well educated. Today, however, if a monk has not already got a degree when he is professed, he may well be sent to university to obtain one later. Several orders maintain their own colleges (the Benedictines have St Benet's Hall at Oxford) in which as much of the monastic life will be maintained as is consistent with pursuing the degree course.

Many monks are already highly qualified when they enter the cloister, and I noticed in the list of monks of Ampleforth, published in the *Benedictine Yearbook*, a doctor of medicine and a chartered surveyor. I don't know whether they are respectively the infirmarian and the procurator (the equivalent of a bursar) but they would seem to be well-equipped for those offices.

Although there are still a few monks who prefer not to become priests, since the Vatican Council in the 1960s lay brethren no longer exist as the second-class citizens that they were in the old days. They are either monk-priests or monks.

The modern plan is not so standard as it was. When the religious started to re-establish themselves in the United Kingdom, they were very rarely able to re-possess even the ruins of former monasteries, although the nuns at Minster in Thanet have reoccupied some Norman buildings. Believe it or not, there was actually a suggestion not all that long ago, that Benedictines might like to refound a community at Fountains. In saying what a loss that would have been to those of us who like visiting ruins, I am reminded of the young lady of County family who returned to see what the Jesuits had made of Heythrop, her former home. When shown the new chapel, she gave a horrified gasp and said: 'What sacrilege! To think that this was the finest real tennis court in England'.

Most establishments had to make do with what they were given, and to build additions when and where they could. Many of the old rooms survive, however, even if not in the same relationship to each other. You could expect to find a refectory, a warming house (still with the only fire – though there may be central heating elsewhere), an infirmary, and perhaps a chapter house, although sometimes the chapter might meet elsewhere, rather than have a whole large room set aside for only spasmodic use. There will be a cloister, although not necessarily one a hundred feet square, but there is unlikely to be a dormitory – except perhaps in the Cistercian houses. I am pleased to learn that the abbot will probably once again live a very similar life to that of his fellow monks, now that he is relieved from the duty of regularly entertaining his monarch or the lords temporal, but he will probably have an office, as well as the bedroom allotted to an ordinary monk.

It may be that much of the above information is already well known to some of my readers, especially any with connections among the religious, but I hope that it may add a little to the knowledge and pleasure of those who, like me, have lived hitherto in ignorance of the modern monastic life. However, I imagine that life for the monks of today is comfort itself compared with that of their mediaeval predecessors, who probably had ill-fitting doors, rarely had windows, and certainly never enjoyed central heating.

Selective Gazetteer

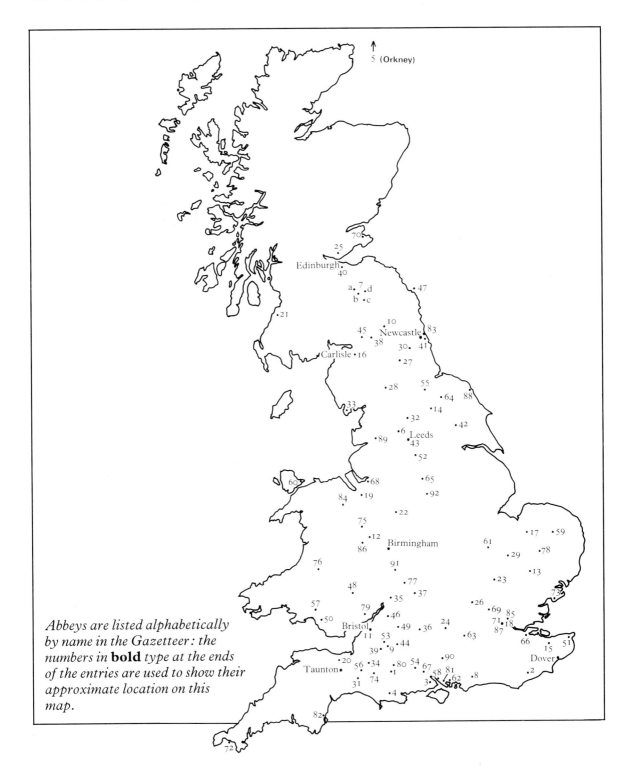

5 (Orkney)

70

25

Edinburgh
40

a 7 d
b c

47

21

10

45
38
Newcastle 83

30 41

Carlisle 16

27

28

55

64 88

33

14

32

42

6 Leeds
43

89

52

60

68

65

84 19

92

75

22

12

17 59

86

Birmingham

61

29 78

76

91

13

48

23

77

37

57

79

35

26

69 85

50

46

71 18

Bristol

49 36

24

87

11 53

44

63

66

15 51

39 9

Dover

Abbeys are listed alphabetically by name in the Gazetteer: the numbers in **bold** *type at the ends of the entries are used to show their approximate location on this map.*

20 80 54 90

Taunton 56 34 67

1 58 81

31 74

3 62 8

4

82

72

Ansty I got there, but it was spelt wrongly. Said to be the best group of Hospitaller buildings, but the hospice is a great disappointment. **1**

Battle Interesting associations with William the Conqueror. Magnificent novices' chamber, equal to most great halls. **2**

Beaulieu Motor cars, too. The parish church was the refectory, and the pulpit was the refectory pulpit. **3**

Bindon Tess's grave, if you like that sort of thing. **4**

Birsay (Orkney) Tidal access to interesting site. **5**

Bolton The ruins aren't up to much, but the setting is beautiful. **6**

The Borders **7**

   Melrose The commandery, and a crude propping-up operation. **a**

   Dryburgh Beautiful setting; interesting night stair and sunken chapter house. **b**

The hospice at Ansty.
Now just a barn, this was the principal hall for receiving passing pilgrims, whom the Knights Hospitaller were instituted to serve – though primarily in foreign parts.

Jedburgh.
The very steep slope forced some unusual arrangements upon the monks. The site has been extensively excavated since this photograph was taken.

Jedburgh Striking nave and extensive excavations cascading down the hill. **c**

Kelso Remains of western transepts. **d**

Boxgrove A lovely spot, with the choir retained as the parish church. **8**

Bradford-on-Avon The Saxon church may be monastic. The great barn certainly is. **9**

Brinkburn A complete church, bare and disused, more like the original than a Victorianised cathedral. **10**

Bristol (Cathedral) Good gateway. Interesting night stair. Superb early chapter house. **11**

Buildwas Handy for Ironbridge. Fine exposed Norman nave arcade, and sunken chapter house. **12**

Bury St Edmunds Very extensive site, but most remains only at foundation level. Two fine gatehouses. **13**

Byland Good example of a lane (lay brothers' cloister). Mediaeval tiles *in situ*. Chapter house lectern. **14**

The water tower at Canterbury. *A complete plan of the water supply here survives. The tower formed a central supply point from which much of the abbey's water was distributed.*

Canterbury **15**
  Cathedral Kinked ground plan. Plan of water supply. Scene of Becket's martyrdom and the pilgrims. **a**
  St Augustine's Monastery The first of the Roman order founded in England. Remains are rather sketchy, but it's what they stand for that counts. **b**
Carlisle Church knocked about a bit, but good refectory, and stone roofed barn. **16**
Castle Acre Twelfth-century west front. Prior's lodging. **17**
Charterhouse (London) Just round the corner from me, but its confused and fragmentary remains leave me somewhat unenthusiastic. **18**
Chester (Cathedral) Well maintained refectory and frater pulpit. **19**
Cleeve Almost complete dorter, with good day stair. Very late frater, with almost complete tiled floor of earlier one. Low-vestibuled chapter house. Little visited, but one of my favourites. **20**
Crossraguel Extensive and interesting lay-out. **21**
Croxden 'The Abbey Church is most unfortunately cut in two by the public road' (Guide leaflet). Chevet. **22**
Denny Hard to disentangle remains, but interesting because occupied by three successive orders. **23**
Dorchester (Oxon) Interesting church. Nothing else. **24**
Dunfermline I really must go and see this apparently (to judge from photos) beautiful church. **25**
Dunstable The remains of a fine west front. **26**
Durham (Cathedral) Magnificent nave; chapel of the nine altars; Galilee; dorter; repeat, magnificent nave. **27**
Easby Extensive remains on sloping site. Adjacent chapel. Pleasant walk from Richmond down the railway line. (I went by car.) **28**
Ely (Cathedral) Entry charge to be deplored: is it a cathedral or a museum? The lantern is unique, however, and there is an extensive range of outbuildings, especially Prior Crauden's chapel with its tiled floor. **29**
Finchale Extensive remains on a picturesque bend

Below: the nave at Durham. *This converted me to an abbey enthusiast. The photograph does not do justice to it. I can only recommend a visit.*

Domestic buildings at Ely.
*There is a wide range of buildings
still standing at Ely, of which
many now house officials of the
cathedral or parts of the King's
School.*

in the Wear.   **30**

Forde I haven't been there, but I believe that the mansion retains some good monastic rooms.   **31**

Fountains Just about everything. The finest lay brothers' undercroft in the country (and on an August Bank Holiday Saturday you might hear a concert by the chamber choir in which I sing). A lay brothers' night stair. Foundations at least of all sorts of ancillary buildings: a mill, guest houses; infirmary; lay brothers' ditto; refectory; chapter house; and a grand church. A *sine qua non* for the abbey enthusiast.   **32**

Furness Rich red buildings, with fine infirmary. Great row of multi-ordered doorways in eastern range. **33**

Glastonbury Romantic. Very long nave plus chapels. The abbot's kitchen. The tribunal. **34**

Gloucester (Cathedral) The cloister: its vaulting, its carrels and, above all, its lavatorium. **35**

Great Coxwell A grange barn belonging to Beaulieu. It belongs to the National Trust, now. **36**

Hailes Some interesting cupboards, indications of the night stair in the thickness of the west wall of the south transept. Pleasant site. **37**

Hexham The most noble night stair. Saxon crypt (and Roman tombstone). **38**

Hinton Charterhouse You can only see the chapter house from the road (A36) but The George, at Norton St Philip, may have been a guest house. **39**

Holyrood Comes on the tail end of the palace tour. **40**

Jarrow Complicated early buildings, including Saxon parts of church. Very good museum fifty yards away. You can take in Monkwearmouth as well. **41**

Kirkham Interesting drainage and sloping site problems. Less frequented than Castle Howard. **42**

Above: a boss from Hailes. *It is hard to appreciate the amount of detailed work that went into an entire monastery. This is one carved roof boss from the vaulting of the chapter house.*

Left: the gatehouse at Kirkham. *Quite a number of monastic ruins are now parts of farms. Kirkham is in fact an English Heritage site, but that doesn't bother the local chickens.*

Kirkstall (As in 'bowling from the Kirkstall Lane end'). Very extensive site. Fine gatehouse, now museum. Large guest house site. More of interest if you're thin enough to slip through the railings.   **43**

Lacock Almost a complete set of ground-floor rooms of the nunnery lurk inside a stately home. You get Fox Talbot, too.   **44**

Lanercost A worthwhile diversion when visiting Hadrian's Wall. The church is still in active use, but the ruins are English Heritage.   **45**

Right : the nave at Leonard Stanley.
The two narrow openings in the south wall are the ends of the staircase which gave access to the rood screen.

Leonard Stanley A very little altered priory church with, in private farm use, a Saxon chapel and a barn with a dovecot in it.   **46**

Lindisfarne Great fun, though the claustral buildings are a bit confusing.   **47**

Llanthony Has a pub inserted in the west front. Very remote, but attracts picnickers.   **48**

Malmesbury Very strange truncating. Magnificent south porch. Guest house now hotel.   **49**

Margam Very simple Cistercian church and west front. The chapter house is through the side door.   **50**

Below: the nave of Llanthony.
That's a pub built into the west end, and when it isn't under snow, this is a popular picnic spot.

Minster in Thanet Reoccupied by nuns, but you can see some of the original buildings. **51**

Monk Bretton Extraordinary site of day stairs. Nice serving hatches. **52**

Monkton Farleigh The well head, or Monks' Conduit, stands in a field. **53**

Mottisfont Another conversion job, but shape of cloister can be seen, and some remains of undercroft (where I have dined). **54**

Mount Grace The only understandable Carthusian remains in the UK. A complete cell (rebuilt); the remains of church, chapter house and cloister, with a very clear layout of cells, gardens and garderobes. **55**

Muchelney Mostly foundations, but interesting Abbot's lodging, and unusual south cloister walk with chambers over. Reredorter block now farm building. Mediaeval tiles in adjacent parish church. **56**

Neath A good lane; the reredorter parallel to the dorter. House conversion makes for confusion. **57**

Netley Interesting conversion into private dwelling, now ruined back to abbey appearance. **58**

Norwich (Cathedral) A lovely church with fascinating roof bosses. Stone vaulted thirteenth and fourteenth-century cloister. **59**

Penmon Norman church, some claustral buildings. Dovecot. On the Menai Straits **60**

Peterborough (Cathedral) Good Norman architecture and many buildings converted to diocesan use. **61**

Portchester Only a small priory church, but you get a splendid castle and magnificent Roman fort in the same visit. **62**

Reading Not very exciting remains, but *Sumer is y cumen in* was composed here. **63**

Rievaulx One of the best. Choir arcades revealed by missing outside walls. Unique chapter house. Splendid frater. Many complications in the infirmary. **64**

Roche Attractive rocky valley setting. Extensive foundations. **65**

The monks' conduit at Monkton Farleigh.
The well head from which the monks' water supply sprang.

The church at Portchester. *Formerly the whole priory stood within the Roman fort, protected by the Norman castle. Now only the church remains.*

Rochester (Cathedral) Super church and some other bits. (And the castle.) 66

Romsey Nunnery church. Refectory unrecognisable in white private house to the south. 67

Runcorn Not much in the way of remains, but excellent exposition. 68

St Albans (Cathedral) Part Norman interior, Roman and Victorian exterior, plus twentieth-century chapter house by William Whitfield. 69

St Andrews Fragmentary but extensive. 70

St Bartholomew's My local. Choir remains in parish use, but choir stalls where they always were: at west end of what remains. Good Norman architecture. Watching loft. I rather like Prior Bolton's rebus (a rebus is a pictorial, frequently punning, representation of a name: Bolton is shown as the shaft of an arrow [bolt] and a barrel [tun]). 71

St Michael's Mount More fun than monastic. 72

St Osyth Gatehouse, and not much else monastic. 73

Sherborne Lovely fan vaulting; remains of claustral buildings mostly incorporated in the school. 74

Shrewsbury Home of Ellis Peters' hero Cadfael. Frater pulpit stands in neglected solitude on far side of the road. One slate on the roof of the church has my signature on it, for which I paid £1. 75

Strata Florida Has collation lectern, but bad weather stopped me from getting there. 76

Tewkesbury Burnt Norman pillars, fourteenth-century vaulting. Fifteenth-century abbot's house. **77**

Thetford Rather unattractive flinty remains, but interesting infirmary. Warren lodge nearby. **78**

Tintern Much celebrated by one of the worst famous poets: Wordsworth. Romantic setting. Northern cloister. Extensive remains. Lay brothers' cloister outside west front. **79**

Tisbury The biggest barn in England(?), and a fine gatehouse, both part of a farm on a minor road. **80**

Titchfield Nave converted into gatehouse of private dwelling. Some mediaeval tiles. Grange barn very nearby. **81**

Torre Almost lost in mansion, but barn survives. **82**

Tynemouth Priory and castle for one entry fee. Percy chantry of fifteenth century. Most of rood screen and part of pulpitum survive. **83**

Valle Crucis Square chapter house with eccentric, not threefold entrance. Upper floor to east range includes dorter and abbot's lodging. **84**

Waltham The nave is almost Durham in miniature. Grave of King Harold. **85**

Wenlock Norman arcading in chapter house. Lavatorium inside cloister garth. Possible scriptorium. Prior's lodging in private ownership. **86**

Westminster Octagonal chapter house. Lots of non-monastic interest. I one lost £70, while I was singing in a service at the abbey. **87**

Whitby Very picturesque, but you need another reason to go there from most parts of England. **88**

Whalley Choir pits. Outlines of octagonal chapter house. Abbot's kitchen. **89**

Winchester (Cathedral) Shrine of my patron saint, Swithin. Fine long nave. Norman font. Converted monastic buildings in diocesan use. **90**

Worcester (Cathedral) Chapter house and refectory in good order. Herb garden in the cloister. **91**

Worksop Truncated nave and good gatehouse. **92**

Selective Bibliography

inistry of Public Building and Works/Department of the Environment/English Heritage Guide Books, leaflets and card guides. I always buy whatever is available in this range, and more than one if more than one is available. It can be very difficult to take everything in from the learned blue booklets, if you've only got limited time on site, so you can use the card guides for a quick tour, and read the blue book later. The more glossy recent publications place more emphasis on photographs, less on text.

Pitkin *Pride of Britain* guides. Usually excellent pictures, but concentrate much more on the living church than the dead abbey aspects of buildings.

The Abbey Explorer's Guide by Frank Bottomley (Kaye & Ward). A really excellent little handbook, in two parts: glossary of monastic terms, covering buildings, orders and practices; and a 'Gazetteer of Religious Houses in England, Scotland and Wales'.

English Mediaeval Monasteries by Roy Midmer (Heinemann). An extended gazetteer, with only a brief general introduction, but giving a short history and an indication of how much remains of all the major abbeys and priories in England.

Mediaeval Monasteries of Great Britain by Butler & Given-Wilson (Michael Joseph). A longer introduction than the preceding book, and a gazetteer shorter in numbers, but very fully illustrated and dealing at greater length with 78 important foundations.

English Monasteries in the Middle Ages by G. H. Cook (Phoenix). One of a series by Mr Cook. No longer in print, I believe, but well worth looking for in second-hand bookshops. A most readable introduction to the different monastic orders, to their buildings, and to their dissolution.

Abbeys by R. Gilyard-Beer (HMSO). A short general guide to the religious and their buildings, concentrating on those in the guardianship of what is now English Heritage.

Mediaeval Monasticism by C. H. Lawrence (Longman). Not about buildings, but useful if you want to know more about the ideas and forms of religious life.

The Benedictine Yearbook, published from Ampleforth Abbey, will tell you quite a lot about modern monastic life in England.

The above books really tell the casual reader all he needs to know about monasteries, but there are many well-illustrated books which may contribute considerably to his pleasure. They include:

Abbeys of Europe by Ian Richards (Paul Hamlyn). This deals at length with twelve major abbeys, including two in England.

Cathedrals and Abbeys of France by Melchior-Bonnet (Larousse). A good general introduction to the subject.

The Monastic World by Christopher Brooke (Elek). A large, glossy, but well worth reading book covering the whole of Europe up to 1300.

The north wall of St Mary's, York.
It was from this monastery, more of which lies beneath the nearby museum, that disaffected monks set off to establish a new community at Fountains.